Being Confirmed

To Hilary

THE RESOURCE ROOM
CHURCH HOUSE
9 THE CLOSE
WINCHESTER
SO23 9LS

Also by Nick Aiken

Working with Teenagers
Prayers for Teenagers
Youthbuilders
Your Life God's Way (Editor)
Day Trips to Heaven

PRESENTED TO

....

ON THE OCCASION OF YOUR
CONFIRMATION

BY THE BISHOP OF

....

ON

.............................19 ....

FROM

....

Being Confirmed

A book for those who have

recently been confirmed

A book for those who need reminding

of the promises they made

by

The Revd Nick Aiken, B.A.

Illustrated by Simon Jenkins

MarshallPickering

An Imprint of HarperCollins*Publishers*

First published in Great Britain
in 1991 by Marshall Pickering

Marshall Pickering is an imprint of
HarperCollinsReligious
Part of HarperCollinsPublishers
77–85 Fulham Palace Road, London W6 8JB

Printed and bound in Great Britain by
HarperCollinsManufacturing, Glasgow

A catalogue record for this book
is available from the British Library

Contents

Acknowledgements

I would like to acknowledge with grateful thanks the help and advice given by a number of friends in the writing of this book. To Canon Tony Chanter, the Rev. Dr Kenneth Stevenson, the Venerable Chris Herbert, the Rev. John Miller, James Jagger and Audrey Swallow.

I should also like to thank the Bishop of Guildford for being so kind as to write the foreword for the book and for providing a lot of helpful comments on the early manuscript.

Foreword

If you have just been confirmed, you will find this book helpful and enjoyable. If you were confirmed some time ago, and things have drifted since then and God seems rather far away or unreal, this book could give you some clues about how to get back on track.

Being a Christian is rather like being on a journey, with all kinds of adventures and uncertainties. You have your map – in the Bible; and you have your food and drink – the communion bread and wine. Nick Aiken has been on this pilgrimage for a while now and in this book he offers many hints about the journey from his own exprience: about how to recognize and keep in touch with God, who is our constant companion on the way.

God does not leave us to get on with life on our own. He asks us to open our eyes and recognize what he has already done. He has given us life. He has moved around in this world as a man and changed it from the inside. He is in action among us now. The adventure of being a Christian is looking for the footprints of God, and scanning the horizon for what he has in store for us.

This book will help to deepen your sense of the presence of God, strengthen your trust and encourage you as you travel on from Confirmation.

Michael Guildford

CHAPTER ONE

God is with us

So you have decided to take the important step of being confirmed. Congratulations! I doubt that you will ever regret your decision because any positive decisions we make about our faith and trust in God only serve to strengthen our belief in him. One of the great statements of the Bible is, 'We love because God first loved us' (1 John 4:19). So as you confirm your faith in public you can be confident that God has taken the first step towards you in offering his love and friendship. In being confirmed you are acknowledging who God is and what he has done, and are expressing your gratitude by putting your faith in the God who can be trusted. Exciting isn't it?

But I don't want to start this book by talking about Confirmation. We will come to that later on. I want us first to look at what God has done for some of the people in the Bible, and then discover what God says to you and me through their experiences. As you know, God used some of the characters from the Old and New Testaments in the most amazing ways. He had a powerful effect on their lives and the lives of those around them. We can learn a great deal from them and they can teach us a lot about what it means to have faith and trust in God. You see, God does not sit idly up in heaven obscured by the clouds; he is a God of action, who intervenes and gets involved in the lives of individuals and groups of people. He is a God who has the power to change things and make things different. He has been affecting the lives of people and whole nations for centuries, and he wants to make a difference to your life and mine.

Case history – Moses

Let's take one individual as an example: Moses. Moses was one of the great characters of the Old Testament. He was born in Egypt to a mother of the Israelite slaves at a time when conditions were very harsh. Because of political instability and the threat imposed by the growing number of Israelite slaves, Pharaoh, the Egyptian king, decreed that all the new-born male slaves should be thrown into the river Nile.

Moses' mother however defied this barbaric law and hid her baby in the bullrushes,

12

hoping that he would be discovered by one
of the Egyptian mothers who could look after
him. It was Pharaoh's daughter who found
him as she went down to the river to bathe.
She adopted him and he was brought up
within the king's family. Moses therefore had
a very privileged background. But his rather
charmed world fell apart when he murdered
an Egyptian guard. Moses really was an extraordinary character and a very unlikely candidate for God to use. He was an Israelite
brought up in the court of Pharaoh – a bit of
an outsider. Then one day he saw an Egyptian guard ill-treating one of his own people,
and in a cold-hearted manner he killed the
guard and attempted to cover up the evidence
by hiding his body in the sand. He probably
thought he was doing his own people a
favour. However, the next day he caught two
Hebrews fighting each other and he tried to
break up the argument. Basically they told
him to get lost, and one of the men said,
'Who made you our ruler and judge? Are
you going to kill me, just as you killed the
Egyptian?' (Exodus 2:14).

Moses had not realized that anyone had
seen his crime and he became terrified
because he knew it would not be long before
Pharaoh would find out what had happened.
So he had no option but to flee the country
before he was arrested. He went far away to

the land of Midian, which is the area between the Gulf of Suez and the Gulf of Akaba. Eventually he got married, started a family and tried to forget the whole episode. The story of Moses might have ended there. He might have been forgotten for ever. But God had different ideas and although we may try to run away and avoid past mistakes, God does not give up on you or me or avoid us, as Moses found out.

One day he was out looking after his father-in-law's sheep when he happened to notice that a nearby bush was on fire. He barely gave it a second glance – except, somehow the bush was not consumed by the flames. It was on fire yet was not burning. God had got Moses' attention! Moses went closer and then God spoke to him. How did he speak to him? Was it in some thundering voice from heaven? It may have been but I doubt it. God probably spoke more through Moses' thoughts. Moses was possibly aware of what God was trying to communicate because of the strength and clarity of what he felt, and the thoughts in his mind. It's not an uncommon experience. Christians often find that God communicates his will to them through their thoughts and their convictions. Ask your Vicar, for example, if he has not already told you, how he felt called to be ordained and if he has ever heard the voice of God.

So God spoke to Moses and he told him that he had seen the sufferings and difficulties of the children of Israel as they were enslaved by the Egyptians, and that he was going to rescue them. This passage from Exodus 3 immediately tells us that God is a God who listens, who is concerned about injustice and who answers the prayers of his people. But all this dramatic and exciting news was not really the sort of thing that Moses wanted to hear. The crunch came in verse 10 when God says:

'Now I am sending you to the king of Egypt so that you can lead my people out of his country.'

The last place on earth that Moses wanted to go was back to Egypt. After all, he had fled for the very reason that his life was in danger if he stayed. Surely God had got the wrong person, because he had committed a murder and was wanted by the Egyptian police. He was a totally unsuitable candidate and he told God so.

Well, God had not got the wrong person. Despite Moses' failure God could use him. The simple truth in Moses' story, and one which is illustrated again and again throughout the Bible is:

GOD CAN USE ANYONE — EVEN YOU AND ME.

I doubt that anyone reading this book has ever got things wrong to the degree that Moses did. Yet God used him, and if he can use Moses he can use you! Don't ever say to yourself, 'I'm not good enough, there is no way God could ever use me.' You should not say it for two reasons: firstly, it is not true, and secondly, God wants to get involved in your life and use you for his kingdom. This is the exciting thing about Confirmation. You are saying to God, 'I mean business. I believe and trust in you and I want my life to count for the things that are important and are of real value.' Confirmation is a new beginning. It is not and never shall be the end where you can say, 'That's it! I've done my bit and observed my religious obligations to my parents and godparents'. That is not it. It is just the beginning of a life that finds a deeper quality and purpose in the service of God and others. And this can be your life. We are faced with a choice, we can either live our life the way we want, which on the surface looks very attractive, or we can live the way God wants.

The amazing thing is that although God's way is more difficult, in that you are asked to live your life to the highest standard that you can, it is ultimately far better because we discover that God will use us in ways that we never imagined. If you think you have big ideas about what you want to achieve in life, you can be sure that God has even bigger plans. God's plans are always centred around the things that really matter and are of true value. As a Christian I look at how God's purposes for my life have unfolded, and all the things that have happened, and I am amazed! The ideas of what I should do with my life that I had when I was a teenager seem quite boring in comparison to what God's plans have turned out to be.

Let's go back to Moses and find out what his reaction was when he discovered the task God had for him.

'I am nobody. How can I go to the king and bring the Israelites out of Egypt?'

In other words, 'Who, me?' You probably could have knocked Moses over with a feather. In fact as the conversation went on you get the impression that Moses was not at all keen on God's plan. He began to raise all sorts of objections. In chapter 4:1 of Exodus he says:

'But suppose the Israelites do not believe me and will not listen to what I say? What shall I do if they say you did not appear to me?'

He then begins to feel very inadequate and in verse 10 raises the point:

'No, Lord, don't send me. I have never been a good speaker, and I haven't become one since you began to speak to me. I am a poor speaker, slow and hesitant.'

In the end Moses gets desperate and simply says in verse 13:

'No, Lord, please send someone else.'

It was quite clear that Moses did not want to go. But God had said something to Moses at the very beginning of their conversation, the impact of which Moses had not fully under-stood. The Lord had said, in verse 12 in chap-ter 3, one simple thing which makes an entire world of difference. It was this:

'I will be with you.'

Moses had not realized it, but what God was trying to say was, 'These are my plans which I want you to carry out and I will be with you as you perform my task'. When God gives us a task to complete during a day or week or month or even a lifetime, he will also be with us and give us the strength and energy to do what he wants. He is not a God who gives orders and then walks off leaving you to do the job on your own. What he does is to work with us. One thing that puzzled me about the Bible for some time was why God seemed to repeat himself so much. Like a needle that had got stuck on a record, the Bible seemed to say the same thing over and over again. God was always telling people he was with them. Look up some of these references and you can see the point I am making.

– Exodus 33:14
– Psalm 16:7 and 8
– Psalm 139:1–18
– Isaiah 49:14–16
– Matthew 28:20

I've come to the conclusion that God says this

so often because we just don't realize how significant it is. We are so slow to realize that it is true. Can you imagine it? We all have moments when we feel let down. Our friends are all out enjoying themselves and we are left behind. But God is with us. We are feeling upset, we did not mean to argue with our parents. But God is with us. We may hate ourselves for something we said or did wrong. But God is with us. He will never desert us or let us go. God's promise is that he will be with us wherever we go, even where two or three are gathered together he will be there. God is not in the business of desertion, quite the opposite, he loves and cares for his children. As a result he is constantly there to lead us and guide us. That is great news for us and it was great news for Moses. But like us he was a bit slow to realize what it meant.

After some straight talking from God, Moses came round to the opinion that he had to go back to Egypt and be obedient to what God wanted him to do. So he did. And what was the result? Well, what took place was one of the most remarkable events in history. God, through Moses, brought the children of Israel out of captivity and oppression, through the wilderness and into the Promised Land. How was Moses able to do this remarkable thing? – because God was with him.

Who can keep a promise?

One of the things we may be anxious about in being confirmed is whether we can keep it up. It is not easy being a Christian, in fact it would be easier not to be. Can we keep the promises that we make? Well you can, with God's help. Because it is he who promises to be with us. All the time he is trying to encourage us and strengthen us for our lives as Christians. Have you ever broken a promise? I guess all of us have at one time or another. We all fail and get things wrong. As Christians we may at times disobey God and forget about him. We may neglect praying, reading the Bible and going to church. At times our personal behaviour may fall short of a good Christian example. But being a Christian is not about pass or failure. Just because we may feel a failure and far from God doesn't mean God has given up on us. Quite the opposite. Who can keep a promise? God can! You see, your Christian faith is not dependent on you, but rather on God and what he has done. God will never let you down. He loves you and cares about you and he is always with you.

But let's face it, we often may have our doubts. Particularly when things go wrong. Then the temptation is to turn round and say, 'Where is God in all this mess?' It's at times

like these that we have to go back to God and
trust what he says, because we can depend
on his promises and if he says that he will
never desert us then he will keep his word.

Case history – Israel

Probably the greatest crisis of faith for the
children of Israel was during the exile. Basically the problem was this. Israel had been
overrun by the Babylonian army in 587 B.C.
Babylonia covered the area approximately
around modern Iraq. Their king Nebuchad-
nezzar had left Israel in a shambles. There
was widespread destruction of the towns and
villages. Thousands died in battle and from
the ensuing starvation and disease.

Considering the magnitude of the tragedy
that overtook the Israelites it was amazing
that they did not disappear as a people alto-
gether. Before the invasion there had been
about 250,000 people living in the land. Sev-
enty years later there may have been only
about 20,000 Israelites left. Thousands of
them were dragged off to Babylon into exile,
and it was there that they became totally dis-
pirited and depressed. Where had God been
when they needed him most? He had led
them into the Promised Land which he had
given them, and yet now they had been
defeated in battle, their land had been ruined

and they were in exile. God had failed them.
In utter despair they said in Isaiah 49:14:

'The Lord has abandoned us!
He has forgotten us.'

I suppose it is probably true for all of us that
when things go wrong and life is difficult we
feel dejected and miserable. But it is at times
like this that it is crucial that we focus our
faith not on our problems but on God.
Because what did God say in reply to the
Israelites and their doubts?

'Can a woman forget her own baby
and not love the child she bore?
Even if a mother should forget her child,
I will never forget you.
Jerusalem, I can never forget you.'

These very powerful words, which the prophet as God's messenger uttered, then gave
the children of Israel a new heart and a new
faith. The comparison that God uses is very
moving. We all know that if a mother aban-
dons her child it is one of the most awful
tragedies in life. A baby is so dependent on
its mother's love and care, and the relationship that they have is particularly unique and
special. However, even the human love of
mother and child can break down. But God
says that his relationship with us, his
children, is even stronger and it will never

fail. That is wonderful, isn't it? We have a God who will never desert us, who will never let us down.

What the children of Israel discovered was that they were asked to live by faith and trust, not by sight. They looked all around them and all they could see was disaster and troubles, and they thought that God therefore had obviously left them. But that was not true. There may be times in our lives when we feel God is particularly close. You may have felt that when you were confirmed by the Bishop, or when you have been to a great service at church. You may have felt it when you have had a special time of prayer or seen something of great beauty. But as we all know, there are times when God seems absent and so far away. These times are usually when life is difficult and painful. But our belief is based on fact and faith and not on feelings. We know that God keeps his promises and it is him we need to trust. So even in the whirlwind of tragedy, if you feel you have let go of God you can be assured that he has got hold of you, and fortunately his grip is far stronger; stronger even than death.

Do you have a favourite Psalm? I guess we all do. My favourite is Psalm 139. All of it is very powerful stuff. One particular section says this:

Where could I go to escape from you?
Where could I get away from your presence?
If I went up to heaven, you would be
there;
if I lay down in the world of the dead,
you would be there.
If I flew away beyond the east
or lived in the farthest place in the west,
you would be there to lead me,
you would be there to help me.

There is nowhere we can go that is out of
the reach of God. There is nothing that can
happen to us that will separate us from his
love and care. As a Christian he has made
you his child and brought you into the most
special relationship you can have. Life takes
on a new dimension because you now know
that you live under the protection of the most
powerful force in life, God's love!

CHAPTER TWO

Jesus of Nazareth

Sometimes I have been privileged to meet people who have done some of the most worthwhile things in their lives. I've also met people who have suffered a great deal yet have overcome the difficult experiences they have been through and shown an amazing sense of life and courage. I always feel I can learn something from these people because each in their own way has something special to offer. However there is one person I've met who really does seem to know what life is all about and who is amazing.

This person never wrote a book. He never obtained a university degree. He had no money. He commanded no army. He wielded no political power. He never travelled more than two hundred miles in any direction. He was executed at the age of thirty-three on trumped up charges and put to death. He is now revered as divine by untold millions throughout the world. Cathedrals and churches stand to his glory in every land. The service of Holy Communion which he began is being celebrated somewhere in the world every minute of every day and every night. The person I'm referring to is of course Jesus.

Without doubt Jesus was the most remarkable person who ever lived. No one has had the impact on mankind that this carpenter from Nazareth has. Yet he did not mount any campaign or use any of the modern means of mass communication. He simply lived a life that was totally remarkable. He was remarkable for what he said and what he did. He healed the sick. He gave the blind people their sight and made the deaf hear. His ideas were totally radical. He taught that we should love everyone, even our enemies, and that is what he did. He forgave those who put him to death.

But he was remarkable not just for what he said and what he did, but he was remarkable for who he was. As Christians we believe that he was not just an extraordinary man but that he was the Messiah, the chosen one sent by God to be our king; that in him we see the perfect picture of what God is like because he was God come down to earth to live among us. Can I ask you a direct question? When was the first time you recall thinking that Jesus was someone special? Was it as a result of something a friend said to you, or through reading the Bible or from seeing how important he was to your parents? For me it was when I was fifteen. At that time I did not believe in God and basically lived my life the way I wanted to. But since I did not believe in God nor did I believe in life after death, I could not find any real point to life. After all, you could get your exams, go off to college, get a job, settle down, raise your children, retire and then die and be put in a large wooden box six foot underground. So what was the point to it all that made life worthwhile and of real meaning? The answer was that I didn't know. Yet I was aware that if there was an answer then God must be a large part of it. The more I discovered of Jesus and what he taught about God, the more sense his words seemed to make of life.

One day I sat down at my desk at school and decided that God must exist, and that the most sensible thing I could do would be to try to follow his teachings. So I did. There was no flashing of lights, angelic choirs or anything like that. In fact the whole experience was very undramatic. But what I did discover, and have continued to do, is that being a Christian brings you into another dimension of life where you discover what it is like to live as a child of God and have a Father who loves and cares about you.

So let us return to Jesus and take a closer

look at who he was and what he said and did.

Jesus the person

There is hardly anyone today who doubts that Jesus as a person really existed, because the evidence is so convincing. Apart from the Bible itself there are a number of other historical sources of data for his life and sayings. You will probably recall from your confirmation classes or from your R.E. lessons at school that details of Jesus' life are mentioned by the Roman historians Tacitus and Suetonius. But perhaps one of the most useful historical references comes from Josephus, who was a Jewish historian writing at the end of the first century A.D. In his book *Antiquities*, he says this: 'Now there was about this time Jesus, a wise man, if it be lawful to call him a man; for he was a doer of wonderful works, a teacher of such men that receive the truth with pleasure. He drew over to him many Jews and also many of the Greeks. This man was the Christ. And when Pilate had condemned him to the cross, upon his impeachment by the principal men among us, those who loved him from the first did not forsake him, for he appeared to them alive on the third day. The divine prophets have spoken these and thousands of other wonderful things about him. And even now, the race of Christians, so named after him, has not died out.'

As we know, the early Christians certainly did not die out. Far from it, they went on and turned the whole Roman world upside down with the message that Jesus was the Son of God who had risen from the dead and was alive. Now Josephus was a Jew who it appears was not very sympathetic to the Christians, so it is all the more remarkable that he documents the existence of Christ and what he did. There is in fact more historical evidence to substantiate the existence of Jesus than there is for William Shakespeare!

The Gospel records themselves form a reliable set of documents for the life and teachings of Christ. Although the Gospels were written after the Epistles, towards the end of the first century, they are careful records of various eye-witness accounts of what people saw Jesus say and do. In fact the reason why the Gospels were written after the Epistles was because the Christians at first could hear about the teachings of Jesus from those who had actually been with him. It was only later, as those first disciples began to die, that there was a need to put their accounts down on paper.

Do you happen to know what is the oldest piece of the New Testament that we possess?

It is a small part of John's Gospel dated as A.D. 130 which was found in Egypt and is now in the university library in Manchester. It is only a small piece of manuscript but it is very significant because it is of such an early date. There are other larger fragments which date later than this, and when it comes to the fourth century we have two excellent manuscripts of the complete New Testament. Unfortunately, our other historical records of the ancient world vary considerably in that some of the documents were written between 400 and 1300 years after the events took place. For example, Herodotus who wrote *History*, the earliest manuscript that we possess, in fact lived 1300 years after the work was first written.

But the important thing is that Jesus is not just another historical figure like Caesar or Attila the Hun. He is not just a memorable religious teacher like Gandhi or a revolutionary like Karl Marx. He is the Son of God who was crucified on a cross, who died and came back to life again, and who is alive today and calls you and me to live our lives the way that God our Father wants us to! You see, Jesus is not someone we can casually ignore or quietly forget about after we have been confirmed. If we believe that he is who he claims to be, the Risen Lord, then it is up to us to follow his teachings because we know that they are right. There has never been and there never will be another person like Jesus. He was unique. God expresses himself in all that exists since he is the creator of everything, but supremely God expresses himself in Christ. So if you want to know God then you need to know Jesus, who was sent by God to show us the Father.

Jesus' birth was not the result of his father and mother deciding that they wanted a child, with the decision being purely on a human level. God intervened in a way that was special and different. It was unlike anything that had happened before or has happened since. This person whom we call Jesus was not just another human being but he was also God as a human. He was God who had come down to earth to live with us. He was the likeness and presence of God here in the world. He is a demonstration of the power and love of God for you and me and for the world which he created and sustains day by day. Jesus is the image of God, so be careful not to focus too much on Jesus as a person without realizing that he is related to and part of God the Father and God the Spirit. If you feel a little confused don't worry, it is a very complex issue, and hopefully when you read the next chapter you will see a little more clearly what the Trinity is about.

Jesus the teacher

Jesus was a remarkable teacher. So much of what he said is very easy to remember, and the stories he told tease you into thinking and wondering what they really mean. A lot of what Jesus taught is told in stories or parables. People would come for miles around to hear him. When he spoke he talked about the ordinary things of life and used them to illustrate a spiritual meaning. Let's take one example.

In Mark's Gospel, at the beginning of chapter four, we find Jesus beside Lake Galilee. On this occasion there was such a crowd that gathered to hear him that he got into a boat and pushed a little way from the lake shore. This provided him with a better opportunity to talk to them. This was the story he told:

'Listen! Once there was a man who went out to sow corn. As he scattered the seed in the field, some of it fell on the path, and the birds came and ate it up. Some of it fell on rocky ground, where there was little soil. The seeds soon sprouted, because the soil wasn't deep. Then, when the sun came up, it burnt the young plants; and because the roots had not grown deep enough, the plants soon dried up. Some of the seed fell among thorn bushes, which grew up and choked the plants, and they didn't produce any corn. But some seed fell on good soil, and the plants sprouted, grew, and produced corn: some had thirty grains, others sixty, and others a hundred.'

And Jesus concluded, 'Listen, then, if you have ears!'

I wonder what the people listening to Jesus by the lake made of what he taught? It appeared simple and straightforward. They were out in the countryside, everyone present, even if they had not actually sown corn themselves, had seen someone else do it. It was a routine part of country living. It seemed simple. But the fascinating thing was, what did Jesus mean by this story? He actually went on to explain it a little later. He told them that it is about the way each of us react when we hear God's message.

Some people will dismiss it immediately and have no time for what God may want to say to them. Other people will initially listen to God's message with great enthusiasm, but after a while they fade away. They did not take the whole thing seriously, they just got carried away with their emotions. Perhaps you have some friends like that? They may have got confirmed last year or the year before, but now you don't see them in church

or at the youth group. It is very sad. Then
there are other people who are like the seed
which fell among the weeds. In other words
they become so caught up in material things
and with themselves, that God gets obscured
and left out. The unimportant things such as
possessions become more important than the
things that are of real and eternal value. But
then there is the seed that falls on good soil
which take root and grows. Its growth is most
encouraging, and some seed bears thirty,
some sixty, and some a hundred fruit. Pretty
impressive! But of course the question is,
which category are we in? This is the very
provocative element to Jesus' teaching in the
parables, it demands the question 'What is
our response?' For you, as someone who has
just been confirmed, is it going to be a 'flash
in the pan' or are you going to allow yourself
to be firmly rooted in your Christian faith?
Will you allow your faith to grow and become
stronger so that your knowledge of God and
your experience of his love enriches your life
as you seek to serve him? The choice is yours
and it is the most important choice you will
ever make. Jesus told a lot of wonderful parables which all have a very rich and powerful
meaning. Set aside some time in the coming
week and take a look at three of them, and
ask yourself the question, What do they
mean? The three I suggest you look at are:

Mark 12:1–9. The Tenants in the Vineyard

Luke 12:16–21. The Rich Fool

Matthew 18:21–34. The Unforgiving Servant

Jesus the healer

The Gospel stories are littered with accounts of incidents when Jesus healed people. Sometimes it was people who were blind, sometimes it was people who were deaf or lame. All who were brought to him he healed. However, there was one particular event when Jesus was in Capernaum. You can read the story in Luke 5:17–26. News very quickly spread around the town that Jesus had arrived, and a crowd gathered to hear him speak. The problem was that there was a terrible crush and the house where he was staying was overflowing with people, so much so that you could not even get through the door. As Jesus was speaking four men came carrying a paralysed man and they could not get in. But they were determined not to be defeated, so they carried the man up the side of the building and literally pulled the roof apart to create a hole big enough to let him in on his stretcher. You can imagine the scene. Jesus was talking away to all the people in this crowded house and all of a sudden dust started falling from the ceiling. Everyone looked up to see these four men ripping the roof apart. It does not record in the passage what the owner of the house felt about all this, but I'm sure he was far from happy! Eventually they managed to make a hole big enough to lower down the paralysed man. It records in the three Gospels where this story occurs that Jesus was impressed by their faith, and he said to the man, 'My son, your sins are forgiven.' Now this was when the trouble started because only God, it was believed, could forgive sins, and the religious leaders who were present thought that what Jesus was doing was blasphemous. In other words he was insulting God by doing something that only God had the right to do. Jesus knew what they were thinking and asked them a direct question, 'Is it easier to say to this paralysed man, your sins are forgiven, or to say, get up, pick up your mat and walk?' No one dared to reply, so Jesus said that he would prove to them that he had authority to forgive sins by healing the lame man. And that is what he did. You can imagine the reaction of those who were present; they were completely amazed and praised God saying, 'We have never seen anything like this!'

The incidents of Jesus healing people in the Gospels are numerous. It was surely little wonder that in only three years Jesus made such a powerful impression on people because he spoke so powerfully and acted so miraculously. The crowd had not seen anything like the things Jesus did, because no one like Jesus had ever appeared before. This must be someone special sent from God!

In this particular miracle, Jesus links the act of healing someone with the act of forgiving them. To heal someone means to make them whole, to make them complete. The paralysed man would not have been complete if Jesus had just physically healed him because he needed to be forgiven his sins as well. Being ill obviously affects someone's physical health, you can see the symptoms of someone's illness often by the way they look. If you treat the illness they will begin to look better. Sin also affects a person's spiritual and physical health. The two areas are very closely linked. Modern medical research has shown that often there is a strong connection between physical illness and deep-rooted emotions such as guilt and anger. And it is Jesus, who is the healer, who wants us to be whole. He looks not just at the outside, he looks at the inside of a person as well. It is not enough to be physically well, we need to be spiritually and emotionally healthy also. This is why at the beginning of the Communion Service we usually start with a time of confession. We ask God to forgive us for all the things we have done wrong, whether it is something we have thought or said or done. We ask God through Christ to forgive, heal and restore us to full health.

Jesus who is alive today

Jesus rose from the dead and is alive today – true or false? Either the resurrection of Christ is true and the most significant event in human history, or it is false and is the greatest lie that has ever been told. How each person confronts this question affects their entire life. Why? Because if it is true then it validates everything that Jesus said about life and about death.

If I were to ask you what some of the most significant events in your life so far have been, what would you say? You might mention some very special and happy events, like places you have been to or people you have met. You might talk about some rather sad things which have affected you, maybe the death of a friend or relative. Possibly something that happened which shocked and frightened you. If we had the opportunity to talk we could probably discuss a whole range of things that have influenced our lives, whether it be people, places or situations and circumstances. But if the resurrection of Jesus from the dead is true it will have far more effect on our lives than anything we are likely to experience. Why? Because it proves the validity of Jesus' claim to be the Son of God. God cannot die. You cannot defeat him, and if Jesus was the Son of God then death cannot defeat him either. It also decisively displays that death is not the end. In fact what happened on that first Easter morning, if it is true, is the most significant event that has ever happened in your life. If the resurrection is true then it affects everything, and on it rests the case for the entire Christian message. As one theologian remarked, 'The outlook for Christianity would be bleak if the resurrection of Jesus was in reality not an historic fact'.

From a scientific view we know that dead men do not rise. The question is therefore whether Jesus' body actually mouldered away in a tomb, or whether the tomb was empty and he had risen? Let's take a brief look at the facts:

Jesus was dead. How do we know this? Well a number of key facts are recorded in the Gospel accounts.

1. Jesus was flogged by the Roman soldiers. A beating by the Romans would have left someone near to death, such was the viciousness of this form of torture.

2. Jesus was crucified on a cross. This was the traditional form of execution in the Roman Empire and was the cruellest and most painful form of killing a man that has been devised.
3. Jesus died earlier than expected, after about six hours or so.
4. Jesus was examined by the Roman soldiers who came to ascertain whether he was dead. If he had been alive they would have broken his legs to hasten his death by suffocation. But the executioners, experienced in their terrible task, discovered he was dead.
5. The soldiers' commanding officer certified Jesus as dead to the governor Pontius Piliate.
6. To make sure that Jesus was dead beyond doubt, they pierced his heart with a spear. It is recorded that blood and water came from Jesus' side. A medical pathologist would take this as a verification that Jesus was in fact already dead.

Jesus was buried.

1. Jesus was buried in the tomb of Joseph of Arimathea, a rich man who was sympathetic to him.
2. Jesus' body was bound and embalmed with grave clothes.

3. A heavy stone was placed at the front of the tomb.
4. The tomb was guarded by soldiers specifically detailed to protect it from body snatchers.

Jesus was dead and buried. End of story. But it was not the end. It proved to be just the beginning, because after that literally hundreds of people claimed that they knew him to be alive again – risen from the dead. These appearances began on the Easter Sunday and continued for six weeks until Pentecost. At first even those who had been his disciples were sceptical and did not believe that he was alive. Over this period of six weeks Jesus appeared to various women, the disciples and, it is recorded, up to five hundred people.

If this is really true then it is the most exciting news that mankind has ever heard. Someone has come back from the dead! Someone has done something that has never been done before. He was not just unconscious or temporarily without a heartbeat. He was dead and now he is alive.

However, some will object and say that he was not really dead and later revived in the cool of the tomb. This has been a popular argument, but it seems conveniently to ignore a great deal of the evidence. As we have already seen, the Roman soldiers at the scene of the crucifixion certified that he was dead, and to make sure, they pierced his side with a spear. They were prepared to swear to the governor that he was dead. Also the question has to be asked, how could a man who had been flogged, crucified, pierced, and placed in a tomb with a very heavy stone door, appear to convince his followers that he was alive and well? The argument has no credibility.

Some people have argued that the Jewish authorities could have stolen the body. But there was a Roman guard on the tomb, and if the authorities, who tried to crush Jesus by killing him, wanted to stop the disciples saying he was now alive all they had to do was to produce the body. But they could not because they did not know where the body was. All the people in Jerusalem had to do was to walk a short distance to the edge of the city to discover for themselves that the tomb was empty. Where had his body gone? The Jewish authorities, desperately trying to stop his followers, could not produce it. Their allies the Romans, concerned to prevent any trouble, could not halt the rumours that were turning the city upside down, because they did not know where his body was either.

The other objection has been that the disciples stole his body and then went about spreading the idea that Jesus was alive. The trouble with this argument is that again it ignores a large part of the evidence. There was a guard placed on the tomb. They were specifically placed there to stop anyone stealing the body. That was their task. Some people have said that possibly the disciples bribed the guards. But this ignores the fact that they were professional Roman soldiers who were on guard, highly disciplined and well trained. If they had failed to carry out their orders the consequences for them would have been drastic. They themselves might have faced execution for disobeying orders. Is it possible that the disciples managed to get around the guard? The answer has to be No.

The other question of course is, if the disciples did take or knew of the whereabouts of Jesus' dead body, why then were they prepared to die for a complete lie? Why, if they knew that Jesus was dead, did they go around telling everyone that he was alive? In fact it is recorded that after the crucifixion the disciples were afraid and disheartened, they did not know what to do. Is it reasonable to think that they would invent this wild story that Jesus had risen from the dead, and then dedicate the rest of their lives to spreading that news, finally actually being murdered for it? It does not make sense. Besides, you might expect one of the disciples who knew that this was all a lie to expose the truth of the story, yet at no stage did this happen. There was no rumour within the Church at any point in time that someone had stolen the body. The reason for that was because no one could have or did steal the body.

Whatever way you look at the evidence for the resurrection, you can only objectively come to the conclusion that Jesus rose from the dead. It may seem amazing, it may seem incredible, but all the evidence points to the fact that it is true. But then of course if God is God why can he not bring his own son back from the dead? Surely with God all things are possible. However, the whole point about the resurrection of Jesus is not that God chose to raise his son from the dead, that being the limit of what God did. The point is that God wants to take every situation and circumstance and transform it for good. If God can change the horror of even death then there is no limit to what he can alter for good. His resurrection power is at work in the world today, seeking to change people, communities, and whole nations towards the cause of truth, love and justice. Signs of that resurrection power are all around us – wherever you see prejudice and hatred giving way to understanding and concern, wherever you see oppression giving way to tolerance and friendship. You may see that transforming power working at home or at school or between nations. God is continuously trying to resurrect good out of evil, hope out of despair, joy out of sadness, and love out of hatred. The resurrection focuses our thoughts on what God is able to do, and acts as a powerful demonstrator of what he wants to do for us, our family, our friends and our world.

The life and teachings of Jesus of Nazareth are without doubt remarkable. No one has ever said and done the things that he did. But he is not dead, he is now very much alive. He is more alive than you and I because he has passed through death and is alive again. For you, as a Christian who has recently publicly declared your faith, you now have the opportunity of strengthening your friendship and knowledge of God. The God who is alive, who is real, who knows you and loves you. You have started on the most exciting and worthwhile friendship that you will ever experience.

CHAPTER THREE

God the Holy Spirit –
Power for living

Have you ever tried to make toast with a
toaster that is not plugged in? Yesterday
morning I tried it. Not intentionally, but I put
the bread in the toaster, pushed the lever
down and went back to my coffee and morning newspaper. After a while I thought it was
strange that it was taking so long. So I went
to have a look and discovered that I had not
plugged the toaster in. A stupid thing to do
but on the other hand easily done. Now, all
the electrical equipment in your home oper-
ates off A.C. mains supply electricity. It's
the power that makes things work. You
cannot see it but you can certainly see its
effect.

As Christians we believe in God who is
revealed as Father, Son and Holy Spirit. In
the first two chapters of this book we have
looked briefly at something of the nature and

work of God the Father and of God the Son. Now we are going to look at God the Holy Spirit. But this is where things become a little difficult, because how do you visualize someone who you cannot see? It's easy to speak about God the Father. You think of a god who is a creator and has authority as king and ruler. It is even easier to think about God the Son, as we simply look at Christ.

But how do we describe God the Holy Spirit? Who is he and what does he do? If we return to our electricity supply we can see the effect of an electric current. It gives the

power for lighting, heat and operating a host of different pieces of equipment at home or at work. If you have had the unfortunate experience of having an electric shock you will also know how powerful 240 volts of current can be. If we were asked in an exam question to describe electricity, what it looked like, its size, etc., etc., I think the task would defeat most of us. But if we were asked to describe its effect then we would have no problem. The same is true in many ways with God the Holy Spirit. It is difficult to describe him as a person but we can see the effect that he has on the lives of people like you and me. In the old days he was usually called the Holy Ghost, which was even more unhelpful because that portrayed a picture of a person with a white sheet over them who went around frightening people.

God the Holy Spirit is a person and should be referred to as such. He should never be spoken of as 'it', for he is the third person of the Trinity. The concept of the Trinity is one that most people find very difficult to understand. Even the great theologians of the Church have argued, discussed and disagreed about the nature of the Trinity. So if you find it difficult to envisage God as three persons then don't be discouraged. It is difficult.

St Patrick, the patron saint of Ireland, used to explain the Trinity by showing people a shamrock. As you know, the shamrock is a

plant which has one stem with three intercon-
necting leaves. It is one leaf yet has three
parts to it. In a very simple way it shows us
something of the nature of God. God is one
person yet with three aspects to his person.
In the same way we also have various aspects
to us. Some people, for example, would see
you just as a school boy or girl. Your teacher
would. But it would be pretty awful if that
was the only part of you there was. Other
people see you as your parents' child, and
that is how they relate to you. Then your own
personal friends see you in a rather different
way. Now the question is, which is the real
you? The answer is, each of them. They all
constitute the various parts that go to make
up you as a person. In a way the same is true
of God. One aspect of him is as a creator,
ruler and sustainer. Another facet is of love
and sacrifice, and yet another aspect is of
power and strength for living.

Let me take just one more example. Water
has the same basic chemical constituency but
can be found in three forms: ice, liquid and
steam. Those of you who do chemistry would
be able to tell us at great length about H_2O.
But whether it comes as ice, liquid or steam
it still has one part oxygen to two parts hydro-
gen. So with God we see and experience different aspects of his person within different
situations and contexts. But it is still the same

one God that we experience. If you think about it clearly, if God is God then obviously he is beyond description. He cannot be summed up in the smallness of our human minds. There will always be many aspects of him that we do not understand. Certainly being a Christian is not about knowing all the answers. Even if we were given the answers to all our questions our mind would not be able to cope with the complexity of understanding that would be needed. At the end of the day the doctrine of the Trinity remains a mystery. However, what we do know is that God has revealed himself as Father, Son and Holy Spirit.

The Bible teaches that the Holy Spirit is to be called God because that is what he is. He is eternal and all-powerful. He is present everywhere (omnipresent) and he is all-knowing (omniscient). So let us now stop and look directly at what the Bible tells us about the Holy Spirit. This is where things become rather exciting, because like the electric charge we discover that the Spirit is about God's power: the power for good, for love, for courage and for living.

The Holy Spirit in the Bible

The references to the Holy Spirit in the Old Testament are not as common as they are in the New, the reason being that the Jewish-Christian faith is about revelation. In other words, it is God who gradually reveals more of himself to mankind, and the climax of that revelation is when God sends his own Son down to earth to show us what he is like. The Old Testament, as well as other religions, gives us various pictures of what God is like, but it is only with the coming of Jesus that we are given the complete picture. That is why Jesus said, when he was in conversation with Philip the disciple:

'For a long time I have been with you all; yet you do not know me, Whoever has seen me has seen the Father. Why, then do you say, "Show us the Father"? Do you not believe, Philip, that I am in the Father and the Father is in me?' (John 14:9 and 10).

Therefore, if we want to know what God is like we need to look at Christ because he is the revelation of God. What was known about God before Christ was incomplete. With the coming of Christ we have a more than sufficient understanding of who God is, because whoever has seen Christ has seen God.

Our knowledge of God the Holy Spirit also reaches a climax with the coming of Christ and the day of Pentecost. This does not mean that the Holy Spirit was standing on the side-lines before Jesus came, but rather we did not know as much about him as we do now.

The first reference to the Holy Spirit is in Genesis 1:2:

> The raging ocean that covered every-thing was engulfed in total darkness, and the power of God was moving over the water.

When the Bible refers to the power of God this can be translated, as it is in many versions, as the Spirit of God. So we see that right from the beginning the Holy Spirit was at work as the power behind the creative processes that were bringing the earth into form. But we also discover from the Old Testament that the Spirit was working in different ways as well. For example, that the Spirit was working through the judges, prophets and kings that God raised up. King David was one such person. We are told in 1 Samuel 16:13 that after he had been anointed with oil by the prophet Samuel, the Spirit of the Lord took control of David and was with him from that day on. The only reason that these great men and women of God were able to achieve the things that they did was because the power of God's Spirit was with them. These men and women were special people, and when you read the Old Testament you of course discover some of the remarkable things they did and how God used them. But the children of Israel looked forward to the day when the Spirit would not just be with special religious people, such as kings and prophets, but would be with everyone. God said that he would give his power to all people and that divine inner strength would be freely available. This he promised when he spoke through the prophet Joel:

> 'Afterwards I will pour out my spirit on everyone: your sons and daughters will proclaim my message; your old men will have dreams, and your young men will see visions. At that time I will pour out my spirit even on servants, both men and women' (2:28ff).

The promise is that the power and strength that you and I need to live our lives the way that God wants will be freely available. Trying to live our Christian lives without that source of power is rather like a toaster that is not plugged in – it does not work.

But let's move on and complete the picture of what the Bible teaches us. What we discover is that when anything of great spiritual significance happens then it is because of the Holy Spirit. One of the great miracles was that of the Incarnation, when a young virgin girl called Mary became pregnant, and the

messenger announced that the child would
be the Son of the Most High God. As you
know, Mary was startled and afraid by what
happened, as any of us are when something
unusual takes place. When she asked the
messenger from God how this would
happen, what does he reply? 'The Holy Spirit
will come upon you, and God's power will
rest upon you.' God was able to bring about
this miracle through the work of the Spirit.
The years after Jesus' birth until he began his
public ministry are the period which we know
very little about. We can only presume that
he spent his time growing up as any other
Jewish boy did. He had brothers and sisters
and learnt his father's trade of carpentry.
Then in the last three or so years of his life
suddenly there was tremendous change of
direction. He began teaching and performing
miracles, and people were astounded at his
power and authority. But what was it that
started his public ministry? It was his baptism. In Luke 3:21 and 22 we read:

> After all the people had been baptized,
> Jesus also was baptized. While he was
> praying, heaven was opened, and the
> Holy Spirit came down upon him in
> bodily form like a dove. And a voice
> came from heaven, 'You are my own
> dear Son. I am pleased with you.'

It was with the coming of the Holy Spirit that Jesus was able to perform the things that he did. Without that power from on high he would not have known where to begin or what to do. The same is true for you and me. If we try to live our Christian lives without the Holy Spirit we will get nowhere. Our faith will seem empty and contribute nothing of significance to our lives. Faith and the church will just be a ritual that we go through without hearing or seeing the reality of God. Everything will be obscure and remote. The Spirit, however, brings us alive and puts us in touch with God. He makes faith real. He allows us to discover that there is a whole new dimension to life in being a child of God. How then do you receive the Holy Spirit and have this strength that allows you to live out your life the way God wants? It's simple – you ask!

Ask and you shall receive

You may be worried whether you will be able to keep the promises you make at confirmation. You can with the strength of the Holy Spirit, and that strength is there for the asking. Jesus himself encouraged us to ask. Look what he said in Luke 11:9ff:

'And so I say to you: Ask, and you will

receive; seek, and you will find; knock, and the door will be opened to you. For everyone who asks will receive, and he who seeks will find, and the door will be opened to anyone who knocks. Would any of you who are fathers give your son a snake when he asks for fish? Or would you give him a scorpion when he asks for an egg? Bad as you are, you know how to give good things to your children. How much more, then, will the Father in heaven give the Holy Spirit to those who ask him!'

So in your prayers ask God to give you the help of the Holy Spirit to live out your Christian life each day, and then you can be confident that he will give you the strength that you need. If life seems difficult, pray that the Spirit will give you courage to keep on going. Maybe things are not easy at home. Pray that the Spirit may help you to be understanding and patient with your parents, brothers and sisters. At school or college it might be difficult to live out your Christian faith with those who may at times be cynical and hostile. Pray that the Spirit will give you the conviction you need to stand up for what you believe.

When the bishop laid his hands upon you he said:

'Confirm, O Lord, your servant with your Holy Spirit.'

The bishop and the Church at that point were praying that you would have the assurance of the Spirit to enable you to live out your Christian life. You can, and God's resources are available to you for today, tomorrow and for the rest of your life.

Power with a difference

At Pentecost we celebrate the coming of the Holy Spirit, which was a remarkable event. The disciples of Jesus were gathered in the room of a house in Jerusalem. They were in a sad and confused state, afraid of the future. Their feelings were quite understandable because their leader had been put to death and they had all fled and deserted him. Yet three days later he had reappeared to them alive. He continued to appear for the next forty days, to various people in different places. Many of the disciples now believed he was the Messiah, the Son of God. But they were unsure of what to do. They had listened to Jesus' teaching and seen his miracles, but what were they to do now he had ascended into heaven? Some of the disciples even thought that they would return to Galilee and go back to their old job of fishing.

However on the day of Pentecost things dramatically changed. In Acts 2:1ff we read:

> When the day of Pentecost came, all the believers were gathered together in one place. Suddenly there was a noise from the sky which sounded like a strong wind blowing, and it filled the whole house where they were sitting. Then they saw what looked like tongues of fire which spread out and touched each person there. They were all filled with the Holy Spirit and began to talk in other languages, as the Spirit enabled them to speak.

The coming of the Holy Spirit was a very noticeable event and for the disciples it made a dramatic difference. After they had received the Spirit their attitude changed. They knew what to do, that they must go out and live their lives for God, and they had now been given the strength to do that. No longer were they terrified of what others might think, but they began telling people the good news of Jesus.

For you and me as Christians today, we may not have such a dramatic experience as the disciples, but it is the same Spirit that is in us and with us. There will be times when God may do some very dramatic things for you and through you. You may receive, like the disciples, the gift of tongues, and witness some special moments when God works very powerfully. However, the most important thing is not just the dramatic events but having the strength to live out our Christian lives day by day – to live the way God wants us to live as loving, caring people.

Power for living

As Christians God promises to give his Spirit to those who ask, and when God makes a promise he does not break it. So you can be confident that you will have available the energy needed to live your life God's way. The Bible also tells us what the Spirit can do in our lives. In Galatians 5:22, 25 and 26 it says:

> But the Spirit produces love, joy, peace, patience, kindness, goodness, faithfulness, humility, and self-control. The Spirit has given us life; he must also control our lives. We must not be proud or irritate one another or be jealous of one another.

This passage shows us the qualities that the Spirit is able to bring to our lives. I think you would probably agree with me that each of these qualities is very important. For it does not really matter what you look like, how much money you have, whether you have a lot of material possessions or not, but it matters more the type of person you are. If you are extremely wealthy but have no sense of peace or joy what difference does all your money make? None of us likes someone who is selfish and greedy, but it is better to be kind and generous. The Spirit can produce in us the qualities that are of real value. What we have to do is to decide that we want to be loving, kind and patient, and then ask the Spirit to let those virtues grow in us. The qualities in the passage from Galatians are called the fruit of the Spirit, but the thing is that fruit takes time to grow. So don't be discouraged if you find that you are bad tempered and impatient at times, or that you cannot find any peace. Being a Christian is not about suddenly becoming perfect, but it is about recognizing what is of real importance, and with God's help becoming the person both he and we want us to be.

Another aspect of the work of the Spirit that enables us to live as Christians is the gifts that he gives to us. You may already recognize some of the gifts that you have. You may be good at a particular sport or subject. We usually are good at the things we enjoy. To have a gift for something, you do not have to be better than everyone else, but it is something you are good at within your own range of abilities. You may have a gift for a particular subject at school but that does not mean you have to come top of the class every time. Every one of us has gifts for certain things, and the Spirit can enable our gifts to grow and develop so that everyone benefits. So what are some of the gifts that the Spirit gives? In 1 Corinthians 12 Paul mentions the gift of service, of wisdom, knowledge, faith, healing, miracles, tongues and the interpretation of tongues. These are just some of the gifts, both natural and supernatural, that the Spirit will give to those who follow him. God has already given you certain gifts, and as you grow in your faith he will give you other abilities, which are not for your own personal use but are for the benefit of others.

CHAPTER FOUR

The Church – Joining the Team

He cannot have God for his Father who refuses to have the Church for his Mother (St Augustine).

What is your church like?

Is it:

a) A great place to meet friends
b) A bit boring
c) Worthwhile
d) Somewhere where it's helpful to go
e) A place where I can contribute something
f) Not very friendly
g) An exciting place to be
h) Something I could take or leave

It is very easy to be critical of church and say it is rather boring at times and the sermons are too long. But church is not about being entertained, it is about being part of a body of people who offer their worship to God. In being confirmed you have made the decision that being a Christian is something that is worthwhile and of value. It is often the case that the really valuable things in life are not always the most entertaining and exciting things. However, even the exciting can become rather repetitive and boring after a time. What was your reply to the above questions? You may have found that you wanted to say Yes to a number of them. Possibly the church that you go to is very lively and active, with a good youth group and a lot of young people involved. But not all churches are like that. Some find things very difficult and need all the support they can get, and that is why your presence and participation is crucial. If, however, your first and only reaction was that church was boring then I think you should look a little deeper at what church is all about. Whatever your reply was, let's begin by asking a basic question.

What is the church for?

Just recently I was away for a weekend with twenty-three teenagers from various parishes, and we were talking about what we felt the church was for. What was its reason for existing and the part that it had to play in life? After a lot of discussion we felt that the church had something of real value to offer to individuals like you and me, as well as to us as a group of people and to the community as a whole. In other words, the church had something to offer to everyone. To you it gives an opportunity to meet with your friends as well as a place to be alone and think. It is somewhere which can be of help and offer support when you need it. It is a place which reminds you of God and where you can seek forgiveness for your sins.

As a family of God's people it offers an opportunity for worship and celebration, where we can bring our praise and prayers to God. It can support our faith by sharing together and enjoying the fellowship that there is as a family. It encourages us and offers us guidance in how we should live our lives, reminding us of the values in life that are of real importance. It is a role model for life and shows us why and how we should help others. Finally the church is a symbol of faith to those in the community and a vehicle to spread the good news about God. It shows people that there are those who believe in God and reminds them that faith is an important part of life and death.

If you add all these things together you can see that the church can be a very worthwhile and powerful body to be part of. But as you can see from the list of the things that these teenagers felt church was for, it shows that it is not just about a building, it is about people. As a Christian newly confirmed, and now fully part of the church, you have your part to play and your contribution to make. Just as you are not perfect so also the church is not perfect. It has its faults and shortcomings because it is made up of ordinary people like you and me. However, working together for what we believe in, it can be a source of strength to us to make us better people in a better world.

How to get the most out of church

When you go to church wear what you like. You do not have to turn up in your 'Sunday best'. It is not a fashion parade. Although I feel I ought to look reasonably smart, I often wear my jeans under my cassock or, if the weather is hot, a pair of shorts. In fact I have seen a bishop wearing shorts under his purple cassock! What matters most of all in going to church is not what you look like on the outside but what you are like on the inside.

Try to arrive about five minutes before the service, so that you have the opportunity to settle down and get into the right frame of mind before the service starts. It also gives you a quick opportunity to say hello to anyone you need to speak to, so that you know that you are among friends. In contrast the worst thing is arriving late for a service. You come in half-way through the first hymn, and the problem is that it takes a minute or two to find out what is going on. You may have missed the notices, and you may feel slightly ill at ease because you can't find the right page in the hymn book, and you may be stuck behind a pillar. That does not help your appreciation of the service. If you can arrive in good time it puts you in the best mood to get the most out of church.

It is also of value to recognize that your mood has a great deal of effect on how much you comprehend of the service. If you have had a really stressful week and were out at a party the night before I doubt whether you will be on your best form on a Sunday morning. Also, if you feel sad or worried it will determine what you feel about the service. So do not blame the vicar if church is lacking in inspiration. It may not necessarily be his fault.

Most services will last for an hour or so. During that time it is impossible not to let your mind be distracted by other thoughts. If your mind does wander, don't worry, it is a perfectly natural thing to happen. Just take care that you do not let your mind wander so much that you don't get anything from the service. During the sermon the most useful thing is to take brief notes on what the vicar says. Aim to write down three things from the sermon. It may just be three sentences, but this will help you to concentrate on the address and it also makes it a lot easier to remember. Can I make a suggestion that might be helpful in making notes, and that is that afterwards you ask yourself three questions:

1. What did I enjoy most?
2. What did I learn?
3. What made me think?

When you leave church there is, however, one thing you must never ever do and that is to say, 'Nice sermon, vicar'. It usually means the person cannot think of anything to say. So be honest. If you found the sermon helpful, say so. If you disagreed with what was said, then say why. Don't be afraid to say what you think. The vicar will probably be delighted that you were paying enough attention to have an opinion. It takes two people to make a good sermon, you and the vicar. He will probably spend a number of hours in his preparation and will try hard in his delivery, so the rest of it is up to you.

Join the team

The other way of getting the best out of church is to get involved. You may already be part of the choir or the youth group. You may help to serve or ring the bells or be involved in some project in the community. Whatever you enjoy doing, if you are not already offering your help then you should join and play your part. You will get more out of church the more you put into it. Being a member of a church is like being part of a team. If one team member fails to show up, then the whole team is affected. You may think that you are not doing anything of importance when you read the lesson or act as a sidesperson or lead the prayers. But you are. You are offering your unique talents and gifts to the rest of the congregation. Some of the best reading and prayers I have heard in church have been done by teenagers. They have often been expressed in such an honest and sincere way that they have provoked a lot of thought and provided much inspiration to many.

Some people will say, and you have probably heard the remark on several occasions, that you do not have to go to church to be a Christian. They are right, you don't. But if you are a Christian and you do not go to church then there is something fundamentally wrong. God says that if we are followers of his then we should set aside a day to worship him. Look what God says in the Ten Commandments:

'Observe the Sabbath and keep it holy. You have six days in which to do your work, but the seventh day is a day of rest dedicated to me. On that day no one is to work – neither you, your children, your slaves, your animals, nor the foreigners who live in your country. In six days I, the Lord, made the earth, the sky, the sea, and everyone in them, but on the seventh day I rested. That is why I, the Lord, blessed the Sabbath and made it holy' (Exodus 20:8–11).

This commandment makes a great deal of sense, because if you and I spent all our time working we would eventually collapse due to exhaustion. It makes sense to have regular times of rest for the benefit of our bodies, minds and spirits. As Christians we celebrate the Sabbath on Sundays, because that is the day that Jesus rose from the dead. It is a holy day, a special day when God tells us we should dedicate the day to him. If we cannot be bothered to spend one and a half hours joining other Christians, to worship God, then we have got our priorities wrong. We are in direct disobedience to him.

Jesus also gave us a command on the occasion when he met together to break bread for the last time with his disciples.

Then he took a piece of bread, gave thanks to God, broke it, and gave it to them, saying, 'This is my body, which is given for you. Do this in memory of me'. In the same way, he gave them the cup after the supper, saying, 'This cup is God's new covenant sealed with my blood, which is poured out for you' (Luke 22:19 and 20).

Jesus' command is that we should break bread and drink wine together in remembrance of his death for us. As a Christian you cannot ignore what the master said. If you want your Christian life to be real, and if you want a friendship with God, then you have got to keep in regular touch with him and stay part of the team.

What's your gift?

What gifts do you have? You may say none. But if you said that, I know you were being rather modest. In the previous chapter on God the Holy Spirit we thought about the gifts that God gives to us. Those gifts can be both the natural and supernatural gifts of the Spirit. If you sing in the choir then you obvi-

71

ously have a gift for music. You may not be the best singer, but that is not the point. When you add the ability you have for singing to the gifts that others offer, then you have a group of people who help to lead the congregation in worship. It is a very important gift to have. If you are a server, your gift is to serve. The assistance that you give to your priest in the sanctuary is also very important. You may be good at reading or speaking or some other aspect of service which is of great value. Looking at the list below, which do you think you could do?

1. Join the youth group
2. Visit the elderly
3. Preach a sermon
4. Help with Sunday School
5. Visit someone in hospital
6. Help to lead a housegroup
7. Arrange the flowers
8. Explain to someone what it means to be a Christian
9. Look after the church boiler
10. Lead a service
11. Support someone with a problem
12. Sit on the P.C.C.
13. Cut the grass in the church yard
14. Join the drama group
15. Baptize a baby
16. Help to organize the church fete

17. Encourage people to give their money to the church
18. Arrange for someone to come and fix the leak in the church roof
19. Support the activities of the church by your prayers
20. Promote concern for social and political issues
21. Ring the bells
22. Sing in the choir

Probably you would be horrified if you were asked to do some of the above items. That is a very natural thing, because standing up in front of people and giving a sermon is rather nerve-racking. However, this is just a list of a few jobs within the life of any church which are important. While there may be some things which you know you could not do, there will be a number which you may feel reasonably confident at tackling. You may not be able to sing a note but you may be very practical, so you could help to look after the church boiler. There is nothing worse than a cold church, so you would be helping all those who came to worship to feel comfortable and warm. An important job! You may enjoy organizing things. This is a very useful gift since there are always things that need to be arranged and sorted out in the day-by-day, week-by-week running of the church. In fact for any church to work successfully it needs everyone to offer the gifts that they have for the benefit of the congregation and community. I will never forget that a few years ago a very elderly lady who lived in the town asked if two members of the youth group could come around and paint her front room. She had very little money so could not afford to pay a painter and she was not very mobile. Anyway, two of the young teenage girls volunteered to help. The elderly lady was thrilled at their kindness and the job that they did. This was a simple example of two girls offering their time and gifts for the benefit of someone else. Apart from getting the job done it also produced a lot of good will and understanding between the young and the old in the town. Remember what Jesus said, 'There is more happiness in giving than in receiving' (Acts 20:35). You have gifts and abilities which you can offer, and it is as you use those gifts for the benefit of others that your abilities will grow and develop. But if you do nothing with the talents you have, then your skills will never be known and you will be the poorer for it, and so will everyone else. It is also important to remember that being a member of a church is not just about doing things with and in church, it is more about the good things you do outside its four walls.

St Paul talked about the gifts that Christians have and in his letters he mentions a whole range of gifts which are given by God. Let's have a look at what he says in 1 Corinthians 12:4–11.

'There are different kinds of spiritual gifts, but the same Spirit gives them. There are different ways of serving, but the same Lord is served. There are different abilities to perform service, but the same God gives ability to everyone for their particular service. The Spirit's presence is shown in some way in each person for the good of all. The Spirit gives one person a message full of wisdom, while to another person the same Spirit gives a message full of knowledge. One and the same Spirit gives faith to one person, while to another person he gives the power to heal. The Spirit gives one person the power to work miracles; to another, the gift of speaking God's message; and to yet another, the ability to tell the difference between gifts that come from the Spirit and those that do not. To one person he gives the ability to speak in strange tongues, and to another he gives the ability to explain what is said. But it is one and the same Spirit who does all this; as he wishes, he gives a different gift to each person.'

As you begin your Christian life the exciting thing is discovering the gifts God has given you. As you go on in your faith God will also use you in many different ways to encourage and support others. God may use you in the gift of healing with the laying on of hands. If this is something that concerns you, talk to your vicar and discuss it with church members. Do some reading on the subject and offer to assist the group in church who pray for people after the service. God may also give you the gift of tongues, like the disciples on the day of Pentecost. This gift is where the Holy Spirit takes your words as you allow him, and speaks in a language that you have not learnt. It is like having a special language between you and God by which you can communicate with him. Although you cannot understand what is said, things are being expressed which are too deep and profound for ordinary words. To pray in tongues is a very refreshing experience. I was first given this gift when I was a teenager and have used it virtually every day in my prayers. It helps me to be more aware of God and it helps me to pray when I have no idea what I should say.

All the gifts that God gives are not earned.

He does not give gifts because we may have been particularly well-behaved or devout. God gives gifts to us, his children, so that the church may benefit and everyone should grow and be encouraged in their faith. The gifts that we have been given are primarily for the benefit of others. As we use and share those gifts they will grow and develop. God may give us other gifts at different times where there is a need to help someone.

This is where being a Christian is very exciting and worthwhile, because if our lives are committed to his service and we want to be used by him, then he will use us. Sometimes he may use us in quite remarkable ways, and at other times in a very gentle and quiet manner. At times I have been very surprised at the ways God can use even me. Just recently I received a letter from a friend I had been at school with. I had not seen him for twelve years. He wrote to me because of a conversation I had with him during my last year at school. In a long talk we had together, I encouraged him to take seriously his Christian faith and continue to live his life the way God wanted. We both eventually left school and went our separate ways. I completely forgot about our conversation until I received this letter from him. He said he had wandered away from God but somehow he had never forgotten what I had said to him.

The result was that he recently had returned to faith and was now trying to live his life in obedience to God. I was amazed, and it reminded me that God can use us to help others when we may not even be aware of it. As we saw with Moses – GOD CAN USE ANYONE – and the wonderful thing is that he can use YOU. And he will use you in the most worthwhile ways if you allow yourself to use your gifts in his service.

During the confirmation service the bishop said a very beautiful and moving prayer which speaks about what the Spirit can do for us and through us. Let me remind you of it.

Almighty and everliving God, you have given your servants new birth in baptism by water and the Spirit, and have forgiven them all their sins. Let your Holy Spirit rest upon them: the Spirit of wisdom and understanding; the Spirit of counsel and inward strength; the Spirit of knowledge and true godliness; and let their delight be in the fear of the Lord. AMEN.

CHAPTER FIVE

Confirmation and its Significance

When you were confirmed what did you feel?

–nervous
–happy
–excited
–calm
–overwhelmed
–a little self-conscious

Most confirmation services are big affairs with a packed church, relatives, friends, church people and of course the bishop in all his splendour. The local press may also have turned up and taken a group photograph of the bishop and all the confirmation candidates. So, much to your embarrassment, you find yourself in the local paper the following week. The service itself may have caused you to feel a whole mixture of feelings. Your classes may have lasted a number of months, so the service was the climax of much thought and discussion as well as a good deal of instruction on the Christian faith. You may have felt happy that you have reached the stage where you are publicly prepared to declare your faith, as well as a little nervous about the future and how you are going to keep the promises you made.

The first thing to remember is that your faith does not primarily depend on you, it rests with God. That is why this book starts with God and who he is and what he has done. If you keep your faith focused on God then you can face the future with confidence, because it is God who loves you and is always with you. If you think that faith is all up to you and depends on how good you are, then you will find things difficult. I know that I frequently fail in my Christian life. At times I am selfish, I cannot be bothered to pray, I do not love others as I ought to and I am not a good example of what a Christian is. The result is that I feel a failure. It is here that you and I have to be careful because often we are tempted to focus our faith on ourselves and think that we are no good, and we could not possibly be real Christians. Being a Christian is not about the effort we put into being good, it is not based on what we do and whether we succeed at it or not. Our faith is based on God and the fact that he is always faithful to us. If we base faith on us the end result will be failure, if we base it on God, he never fails. Christians often speak about the 'Grace of God'. Grace means the overwhelming love and forgiveness that God shows to us despite the fact that we do not deserve it. We cannot earn God's grace and favour by trying to be good, but rather he gives his love to us out of his graciousness which is a free gift.

When you were confirmed I am sure that you were determined to keep to the promises you made. You were full of confidence. But life can be very difficult and the good intentions can at times get swallowed up with other pleasures. We can get distracted by all sorts of things which tear us away from the path of being a Christian disciple. When this happens we need to come back to God, ask his forgiveness, forget about our failure and direct our faith again to the friend who never rejects or fails us.

Facing the future

Let's briefly in this chapter look at the confirmation service and the promises that you made, and the effect that has on your future.

In the church it is only a bishop who confirms people. This has been the tradition of the church and is for basically two reasons. Firstly, because confirmation is an important event, where you acknowledge that you are a follower of Christ. Secondly, the role of the bishop displays that you are part of the worldwide Church of God. You are not just confirmed into the church of St Mary's or St Peter's, or wherever you happen to worship, you are part of the church in your deanery, your diocese, your country and your world. The bishop represents the unity of the Church of God here on earth.

Laying on of hands

The bishop lays his hands upon you to confirm you. The laying on of hands is a very powerful sign and action that has been part of the Christian practice for two thousand years. What then is the point of the laying on of hands and what does it mean? Let's look at the background of the ritual to see whether we can uncover something of its meaning and significance.

One of the early references to the laying on of hands in the New Testament is in Acts 8:14–17. This passage is similar to the meaning that ritual has at confirmation so let us look at it.

The apostles in Jerusalem heard that the

people of Samaria had received the word of God, so they sent Peter and John to them. When they arrived, they prayed for the believers that they might receive the Holy Spirit. For the Holy Spirit had not yet come down on any of them; they had only been baptized in the name of the Lord Jesus. Then Peter and John placed their hands upon them, and they received the Holy Spirit.

In the New Testament the action of the laying on of hands is used in three ways: to pray for someone's healing, to commission a person for service in the church, and also as a special prayer in a particular situation. For your confirmation the laying on of hands was for the last two reasons: to commission you for a life of Christian service, and, like the passage in Acts, a special prayer that you might receive the Holy Spirit's strength and power to live your Christian life. This does not mean that you did not previously receive the Spirit at your baptism. But rather the church's prayer is that the presence of the Spirit in your life should be confirmed and that you should be filled with that same Spirit of God. As we go on in our lives we need continually to be filled with the Spirit and this should be our prayer day by day. The laying on of hands is also a sign of blessing, and the bishop blesses you in the name of God. It is also a physical touch and an expression of love and care from your father in God. In some ways it is similar to shaking hands or embracing someone. Both are expressions of warmth and friendship. When hands were laid on you the bishop used your name because the sign of blessing was for you personally and you replied 'Amen'.

Promises renewed

When you were baptized as a baby your parents and god-parents made a promise of faith on your behalf. You will not remember anything of your baptism because you were probably only a few months old, though relatives may take great delight in reminding you that you either cried all the way through the service, or were good as gold. At your confirmation you expressed your own faith and trust in God, and completed the promises made for you at your baptism. Your parents and god-parents have undoubtedly prayed regularly for you over many years, that you would grow up to have your own faith. Confirmation therefore is also a result of prayer and your own declaration of faith is answering those prayers. That in itself is a cause of great celebration.

In declaring before God and the church the

faith into which you were baptized you were doing four basic, but crucial things, which are the A, B, C, D of faith.

A – Admit

You were admitting that you are a sinner. In other words, that you have done things wrong. A sinner is someone who is not perfect. None of us is perfect. It is important that we admit to God that we have at times failed to live up to the standards that he has given to us. Because God is holy he hates the sin that spoils us and spoils our world. That sin destroys friendships, families, communities and nations when, through greed and selfishness, people choose to go their own way and ignore God. If we admit our sin and that we have failed, then there is an opportunity that we shall be forgiven and that our relationship with God can be restored. For this reason the bishop asked you

Do you repent of your sins?

You then replied:

I REPENT OF MY SINS.

You then went on to say:

I RENOUNCE EVIL

You are saying in these two statements that you turn your back on all the things which are contrary to the way of love that God has called you to follow. It has been said that for evil to triumph it only takes a good person to do nothing. By renouncing evil you are not just rejecting what you know to be wrong but are saying that you will try to defeat evil by doing good.

B – Believe

What you believe is very important, because it affects the type of person you are. If a person believes things which are wrong, then they behave wrongly. If someone thinks it is acceptable to put their own interests before those of anyone else then that person will be unco-operative and difficult to get on with. At school or at home that can make life very hard, but if that person is in a position of responsibility the results can be disastrous. Hitler or Stalin would be two examples of people whose beliefs were evil and resulted in suffering on a terrible scale. By contrast, if someone believes in love and generosity then usually their life reflects those values.

The Bible teaches that 'God is love' (1 John 4:8). Therefore as Christians who believe in God we believe that love is the most powerful and effective way to solve our problems and conduct our lives.

Being a Christian is not, however, just about believing that we should be good, it starts from what we believe about God. It is very important not to make this mistake. It is a common belief that, providing you behave in a decent manner and do not harm anyone, then that makes you a Christian. It does not. You cannot put action before belief. It is not what we do that makes us acceptable to God, but the fact that we believe and put our trust in him. For this reason the bishop asked you:

Do you believe and trust in God the Father, who made the world?

You then replied:

I BELIEVE AND TRUST IN HIM

He then asked:

Do you believe and trust in his Son Jesus Christ, who redeemed mankind?

You replied:

I BELIEVE AND TRUST IN HIM

And thirdly the bishop asked you:

Do you believe and trust in his Holy Spirit, who gives life to the people of God?

And you said:

I BELIEVE AND TRUST IN HIM

Finally, because our belief in God unites us

in the body of Christ here on earth with all
who trust in God, the bishop said:

This is the faith of the Church

And the whole congregation together replied:

THIS IS OUR FAITH.
WE BELIEVE AND TRUST IN ONE GOD,
FATHER, SON, AND HOLY SPIRIT.

If we say that we believe in God it does not
mean that we believe all of the Bible or know
all the answers. It does mean, however, that
we simply believe that Jesus died for us, that
God is the supreme authority in everything,
and that the Holy Spirit is the gift given to us
as a sign that we are a child of God.

C – Commit

During the time of your Christian life up until
this point, and especially in your confirmation classes, you have been considering
the claims of Jesus Christ on your life. You
know that he has called you to follow him
and commit your life to his service. This is
not just part of your life, it is all of it. You
cannot say, 'In my spiritual beliefs I am a
Christian but I make up my own mind when
it comes to my attitudes and the values by
which I live'. The Christian life is a life of
complete commitment to God. This does not
mean that we have to go and live in a convent

or monastery, but it does mean that we should try to bring our Christian principles into every situation and circumstance that we find ourselves in. Whenever you have a decision to make or are faced with the question of what to do, stop and ask yourself what Jesus would have done if he faced the same situation. When you have thought as to what Christ would have done, then that is what you should do.

The Christian life is one of commitment and that commitment can be very costly. Some people stopped following Jesus because they found what he said very difficult and demanding. Look at what Jesus said on one occasion in Luke 14:25–27:

> Once when large crowds of people were going along with Jesus, he turned and said to them, 'Whoever comes to me cannot be my disciple unless he loves me more than he loves his father and his mother, his wife and his children, his brothers and his sisters, and himself as well. Whoever does not carry his own cross and come after me cannot be my disciple.'

God demands all of our love and commitment because he is totally committed to us. Although inevitably in our relationship with God we will be aware that his love for us is far greater than the love we can show to him, none the less we are called to a life-long commitment, where God and his service should be our first priority. Our love for him should come before our love for our family, our friends and ourselves. Ironically, the best way we can express our love for God is by loving our family, friends and ourselves.

D – Do

We have seen in the previous chapters of this book that God is a God of action. He is a God who speaks to people, who delivers whole nations out of slavery, who sends his Son down to live among us, and who gives the power of his Holy Spirit to those who ask. God's action comes from the concern that he has for everyone. This does not mean that he shelters you or me from difficulties or suffering, but that he gives us the strength to live with the painful things of life. He does not offer an easy way out, rather he offers a helping hand through the problems we encounter.

The bishop, after he has asked you to declare your faith, invites everyone to acknowledge the help that God gives when he says:

Our help is in the name of the Lord

Then everyone responds:

WHO HAS MADE HEAVEN AND EARTH

For our faith to be real it involves action, in other words *doing* something about it. This is why you have to make a personal and public response of faith. St Paul in Romans 10:9 reminds us that it is a matter of not just believing but of actually confessing that Jesus is Lord. In other words, say what you believe. St James in a letter says this:

> Do not deceive yourselves by just listening to his word; instead, put it into practice (1:22).

If you have faith in God you have got to do something about it, and the great challenge is to let it show by the way we live our lives.

CHAPTER SIX

A Friend's Gift – Holy Communion

A few years ago I heard a rather sad story, which was all the more sad because it was true. It involved a very young boy who was sensitive about his mother's hands. The problem was that his mother, who was a very attractive woman, had very nasty hands; they were red and badly marked and scarred. Unfortunately, as a result the young lad did not like his mother touching him and would refuse to hold her hand on the way to school or be cuddled and held. One day his father decided that the time had come for him to tell his son about his mother and her hands, so he took him aside into the kitchen. He gently explained to him that a few years previously, when he was just beginning to crawl, his mother was with him in the lounge when the phone rang. She went out of the room to answer the call quickly, but unfortunately the

message went on longer than she had antici-
pated. Half-way through the conversation
she heard a terrible scream from the lounge.
She rushed in to find that the boy had craw-
led up to the fire place and pushed away the
fire-guard, and his clothes had begun to catch
alight. In desperation she looked around the
room for something to put the flame out with.
She could find nothing. So she grabbed him
and smothered the flames with her own bare
hands. As a result her hands were perma-
nently marked and scarred.

When his father first told him the truth
about his mother and her hands the boy did
not say anything. What could he say? But as
time went on his feelings about his mum and
her hands changed. He began to feel proud
of her hands because he realized that they
were a visible demonstration of her love for
him.

When we look at Jesus on the cross, what
do we see? We see his hands and his feet.
Pierced and tortured. Covered in blood. Dem-
onstrations of his love for you and me. If you
ever doubt, for whatever reason, that God
loves you, look at Jesus on the cross and there
you will be reminded of what lengths Christ
was prepared to go to prove his interest and
concern for you. You have probably got some
really good friends, who you enjoy having
fun with and who you may spend a lot of

time with. But do you think any of your friends would be prepared to die for you? Or let me put it another way, would you be prepared to die for any of your friends? Think about it for a moment or two.

Christ as your friend was prepared to die for you

It is remarkable, isn't it?

Jesus, in case we forgot what he did for us on the cross, gave us the Service of Holy Communion as a reminder of the cost of his friendship. He gave us the bread and the wine as visible signs of his body and blood, which were given for us.

The Service of Holy Communion is the most important act of worship we as Christians have. It is more important than a youth service, or family service or morning prayer or any big celebration that we may go to. Holy communion is the one and only service that Jesus himself gave to us. It is a very moving and powerful act of worship, which no Christian can get bored with because it is full of so much mystery and meaning.

Let me give you a word of warning. It is very easy to think that other churches are so much more exciting. Their services seem to be so much more lively, they have great music and you come away feeling really good. Take care, because worship is not all about getting emotional kicks. You must never judge the value of your church and its services by what it makes you feel like. The most complete act of worship is the Service of Communion. You can find that the service, which your church may call the Eucharist, or the Lord's Supper or the Mass, has so many different layers of meaning that you can *always* get something of spiritual value from it.

A Communion Service can be celebrated anywhere and in a whole variety of circumstances. It can be celebrated in a field, in a house, in a barn, on a ship and even in church. A communion can take place at a wedding, a funeral, at a confirmation, or at any event of thanksgiving to God. The service itself has so much in it and carries so much significance as an act of love and sacrifice of a friend, that you cannot come to the end of its meaning.

Let's celebrate

Although you have recently been confirmed you may have received communion before that event under special circumstances. Whether taking communion is a new experience or something you have been doing for some time, let's take a brief look at this wonderful act of praise and worship.

We begin the service by reminding ourselves of a crucial truth and that is why the vicar says;

The Lord is here

and the whole congregation replies:

HIS SPIRIT IS WITH US

As you read in the first chapter, God continually reminded his children that he was with them and that he would never desert them. When we come together to worship God we can be confident of his promise that he is with us, and he is particularly so when we come together, whether we are young or old, it makes no difference. This is a cause for celebration. But the Communion Service is well thought out. It builds up to a climax. We begin by proclaiming God's presence with us, and then move gradually closer and closer to the most important act of breaking of bread at the end. So we should not rush but take time to draw near to what our God offers to us in the sacraments.

God knows

This is a phrase that many people casually use, often without thinking about it. However, the truth is that God knows each one of us personally. He knows our thoughts and words and actions. At the beginning of the Communion Service we remind ourselves of this fact by saying together this beautiful prayer.

ALMIGHTY GOD,
TO WHOM ALL HEARTS ARE OPEN,
ALL DESIRES KNOWN,
AND FROM WHOM NO SECRETS ARE HIDDEN:
CLEANSE THE THOUGHTS OF OUR HEARTS
BY THE INSPIRATION OF YOUR HOLY SPIRIT,
THAT WE MAY PERFECTLY LOVE YOU,
AND WORTHILY MAGNIFY YOUR HOLY NAME;
THROUGH CHRIST OUR LORD. AMEN.

This is a very moving prayer. I suggest that you read it through once, and then read it again but pausing at the end of each line to reflect on its meaning. The important thing about prayers such as this, is that they act as a reminder of who God is and who we are. They can be fresh to us as a prayer each time we read them because we bring ourselves to God each day and each week with new thoughts and different situations and circumstances.

Lord I'm sorry

We then move on to a time of confession, and we recall that the first and greatest command is that we should love God with everything that we are and everything that we have. However, the truth is that none of us could claim that we have done that. We are then reminded that we should love our neighbour as much as we love ourselves. Again we could rarely say that we have shown that same amount of interest and concern for others as we have towards ourselves. It is not that God and the church are trying to make us feel complete failures, but that our Father in heaven has given us the most important and worthwhile challenge in life. If you aim for the best things in life the chance is then that you will direct your energies to the things of real value. You may not succeed all the time but that does not matter. What matters is that you tried.

We do not need to feel a continual failure because God offers us forgiveness, even though we have not loved the way that we should. It may be helpful, before you come to the service, to spend a minute or two giving some thought to any unkind or selfish things that you have said or done during the week. When you then say the words of the confession recall what you want to seek God's forgiveness for. The Prayers of Penitence will then have a reality and meaning to them which will help to focus your thoughts each time you say them. The great thing is that if we confess our sins and mistakes to God then he promises that he will forgive us. This is why after the confession the vicar pronounces God's forgiveness to us. When God forgives he does not put our sin in a file as a permanent record against us. When we confess our sins it is like writing them on a card and giving it to God. He then, rather than putting it in a drawer marked with your name, tears the card up and throws it away. He forgives and forgets. With some people, if you do something wrong, they mentally catalogue your mistake and then use it as evidence against you at a later date. God never does that. Take a look at these lovely words from Psalm 103:8–12:

The Lord is merciful and loving,
slow to become angry and full of constant love.
He does not keep on rebuking;
he is not angry for ever.
He does not punish us as we deserve
or repay us for our sins and wrongs.
As high as the sky is above the earth,
so great is his love for those who honour him.

As far as the east is from the west
so far does he remove our sins from us.

That is wonderful news, and our response to
the fact that God is prepared to give us a
fresh start should be one of praise and
thanksgiving. For that reason the service gen-
erally follows with the Gloria, which of course
begins with the words:

Glory to God in the highest,
and peace to his people on earth.

We have so much to be thankful for because
of the love that God shows to us. You may
sing this song in your church, or you may
say it. But whatever you do, enjoy the words
and let them remind you that God is to be
revered and held in awe and respect.

Listen, reflect and learn

The next part of the service is known as the
ministry of the word. We have remembered
that God is with us. We have asked forgiveness for our faults and received his pardon,
so now we listen to what God may say to us.
Part of the way you can listen to God is by
hearing the reading of the Bible and by someone explaining what it means. As you listen
to the passages being read try to remember
just one thing about it, and throw it around

in your mind. If it is a story of an incident in the Gospels try to imagine the scene. If this causes you to daydream a little, do not worry. It is far better to remember just one thing rather than madly trying to remember as much as possible and then failing.

When it comes to the sermon, as I have previously suggested, it might be helpful to take a piece of paper with you to scribble down a few notes. You might write just three words that struck you during the sermon. Think about the words in the context of what was said during the address. That will help you get maximum benefit from what is said, and will allow God to impress upon you whatever he may want to say to you through the passage. If you listen and reflect on any passage or any sermon that you hear, you will learn something from it. If a reading or an address seems boring, half of the reason for that will be because of you. It takes two people to make a good sermon – you and the vicar.

A clergyman I used to know had been a professional musician before he was ordained. He said that you could always tell how successful a concert would be by the atmosphere when you walked into the concert hall. If you came in and everyone was shuffling around and not really concentrating, then you knew that things would not go well. But if you came in and the audience were anxiously waiting in anticipation of the music, then you knew that the concert would be a great success. This was because the audience would draw out the music from the orchestra. It is very similar with a sermon or reading. You can always gain something if you are willing to listen and learn. It makes things far less boring!

Next comes the Creed. This comes from the Latin 'credo' which simply means 'I believe'. The Creed is a statement of truth which we declare as being what we as Christians believe. It is a shortened form of all that the Bible teaches about God.

Following on from the Creed are the prayers. Chapter eight is all about prayer, but prayer is not just about you and me as individuals talking to God. It is also about joining together with other Christians and praying. The prayers in the Communion Service cover a whole range of concerns: the church and the world, families and friends, all the things that affect our lives and those of other people.

To go back to the music world, a single instrument such as a violin can be very good, but a whole orchestra of instruments has a depth and richness which is very powerful. The same is true with prayer. It is very helpful to pray on your own, but it can be of greater significance and strength when Christians pray together.

Let's get things straight

The next prayer which we all say together is the prayer of Humble Access. Nothing to do with credit cards but to do with acknowledging who we are and who God is. This is another wonderful prayer, and it reminds us that we have nothing to offer to God. We are not doing him a favour by turning up to church and taking communion. Rather God invites us to come to his feast. We have not earned the right to a place at his table, but because he cares for us he asks us to come and be fed and strengthened. In this prayer there is some straight talking, where we admit that we are not worthy, but despite that God still asks us to come and receive. This prayer is all about being honest with God.

Then follows the peace, where we may greet our neighbour either by shaking their hand or embracing them. The peace is a part of the service in which we recognize that as Christians we are brothers and sisters together. We are part of the one family of God. We are all children of the same heavenly Father. It does not matter what age we are or what we do, we as Christians have a common bond together.

Bread and wine

We now come to the climax of the service: the breaking of bread and the sharing of wine. But I do not want to tell you about all the very important technical implications of this part of communion. I suspect the vicar in your classes looked at the eucharistic prayers that are said over the bread and wine, and explained the significance of all that is expressed. Instead I want to tell you a story.

Many years ago the Archbishop of Paris was preaching at the cathedral of Notre Dame. It was Easter Day and the church was packed with people who had come to worship. The Archbishop in his sermon told the story of three young lads who one Saturday were messing around the streets of Paris. They were a little bored and not sure of what to do. Eventually they wandered into the cathedral, watching the tourists who had come to visit the magnificent building. As they were standing at the back, one of the boys had a rather wicked idea. He dared his friend to go up to the front of the cathedral and into the confessional box and tell the priest as many awful and terrible sins as he could possibly think of. At first the boy was a little unsure about whether he thought this was a good idea or not. But encouraged by his two friends he decided to accept the dare.

He walked up to the front, found a confessional box and went inside. I should say, in case you do not know, that the confessional box is a small cubicle where you can privately talk to the priest and admit to your sins. After a few moments of hesitation he began to tell the priest the most dreadful sins he could imagine. For about twenty minutes the priest said nothing while he told one lie after another. Each time the sin that he could think of became more outrageous. Eventually he stopped, unable to think of anything else to say.

The priest did not say anything at first, but after a long pause spoke up. 'I want you to walk out of the confessional and go and stand before the great cross above the high altar, and I want you to look at Christ on the cross and say, "You died for me and I don't give a damn!" ' The boy at first felt very nervous because he realized that the priest had understood what he had been doing. He stepped out of the confessional, and part of him wanted just to run out of the cathedral and forget about the whole thing. But somehow he felt compelled to do as he was told. He went up to the altar and looked at Christ on the cross. He saw this tortured and dying figure and began to speak the words, 'You died for me and I don't give a damn'. But before he reached the end of the sentence he was overcome with tears as he realized the truth of what he was saying. The Archbishop finished his sermon by saying, 'I know this story is true because I was that boy'.

When Jesus met with his disciples the night before he was crucified he shared the Passover meal with them. But he gave this ancient ceremony, which remembered the children of Israel's deliverance from Egypt, a new meaning. In the breaking of bread he said to his disciples, 'Take, eat; this is my body which is given for you; do this in remembrance of me.' He then took the wine and said, 'Drink this, all of you; this is my blood of the new covenant, which is shed for you and for many for the forgiveness of sins. Do this, as often as you drink it, in remembrance of me.'

When Jesus died on the cross he did so for you and for me. Unless we understand what this means, Christianity just remains a cold, dull religion. But like the boy in the story, when we personally discover this was an act of love done by a friend because he was prepared to take the consequences of our sin, then our lives will never be the same again. When we come to take the bread and the wine in gratitude for the love that Christ shows to us, our only response can be to live our lives after his supreme example.

Gratitude should inspire us so that in all we do and say we do it out of thanks to our greatest friend.

At the end of the Communion Service we join together in a very moving prayer of thanksgiving, and when you say it in church use all the emotion you have. Don't let familiarity dull the sense of appreciation you should express to God for what he has done for you. Read it slowly as it is written below and allow the meaning of what is expressed to capture your thoughts and imagination.

ALMIGHTY GOD,
WE THANK YOU FOR FEEDING US
WITH THE BODY AND BLOOD OF YOUR SON
JESUS CHRIST.
THROUGH HIM WE OFFER YOU OUR SOULS
AND BODIES
TO BE A LIVING SACRIFICE.
SEND US OUT
IN THE POWER OF YOUR SPIRIT
TO LIVE AND WORK
TO YOUR PRAISE AND GLORY. AMEN.

CHAPTER SEVEN

The Bible – Words of wisdom

Do you know what is the best-selling book of all time, and the book which is consistently top of any best-seller list? The answer is the Bible. No other book has had such a profound effect on people and whole nations as the Bible. In some countries of the world the Bible is reckoned to be such a powerful and danger- ous book that it is banned, and Christians have to go to great lengths to smuggle it into the country. We are very fortunate that we can go into any bookshop and buy a copy without any difficulties. Our problem is that we tend to take it for granted, but if we want to grow in our knowledge and understanding of God then it is important that we regularly read the Bible.

Many hundreds of years ago there was a famous saint called Augustine who was bishop of Hippo in north Africa. One day he was walking along the beach and he happened to notice a small boy digging a hole in the sand. He did not pay much attention to him, except that after a short while the boy started walking down to the sea, filling his bucket up with water and emptying it into his hole. The boy kept on doing this, until Augustine became curious as to what he was trying to do. So Augustine asked the boy and he explained that he was trying to empty the sea into his hole. St Augustine gently laughed and told him that the sea was so vast and so great that he could not empty it into his hole. As Augustine walked away he realized that in fact God is so vast and so great that we as mere human beings can never understand him. Our minds are so small that we cannot possibly contain a knowledge of someone who is obviously so big and powerful. It was then Augustine realized that the only way we can know anything about God is if God shows himself to us. The good news is that, through Jesus, God does show us what he is like, and our understanding of God comes from the Bible. This is why the Bible has always been such a powerful book. It is a book inspired by God. It is not just a collection of stories and wise sayings but it is a book in which God himself is trying to communicate to us.

The Bible is not just one book, it is in fact

sixty-six short books that make up a collection. It was written by many different people at different times over hundreds of years. Originally it was written in Hebrew and Greek, with some parts in Aramaic. It also contains different types of literature. Some is poetic, like the Psalms which is a collection of a hundred and fifty pieces of poetry. Some parts are simply stories of people and their experience of God, such as the book of Genesis. Then there are books which are mainly legal and ritual instructions, like the book of Leviticus. Other books are called prophetic because they are an account of the words of warning of a particular man or woman of God, to the children of Israel. Then some books are a collection of wise sayings which people found to be very helpful. An example of this would be the book of Proverbs. Other books which are very difficult to understand are about the future, and they are a collection of wonderful visions and pictures. The best example of this is of course the book of Revelation. There is also a collection of what is called the Epistles. The word 'epistle' simply means 'letter', and these are various letters that either St Paul or St Peter or possibly another saint wrote to a church or an individual. Then there are the Gospels, Matthew, Mark, Luke and John, which are a rather different type of literature. The word gospel means 'Good News', and these four books tell the good news of the coming of Christ the Messiah.

So the Bible is an amazing collection of all different types of literature. Some parts are very easy to understand and some are very difficult, so in making a regular habit of reading it it is best not just to begin at Genesis and read right through to Revelation, but rather to start with a particular book. In a few pages we can look at how to read the Bible, but before that let me ask you a question. . . .

Why read the Bible?

Is it important for you as a newly confirmed Christian to read the Bible? Yes. But you may say, 'Why? I can get by perfectly well without reading it'. Let me suggest just four reasons why you should take the time to read your Bible regularly.

The Bible can guide you

What type of person do you want to be? I'm not talking about what you hope to achieve or what career you want to follow, but rather what kind of person you want to become. Do you want to be someone who thinks only of themselves or someone who actually cares about others? Do you want to be someone who does only what they want or someone who considers the views and opinions of others? You will I'm sure say, 'Of course I want to be kind and thoughtful and generous. I want to be a good person.' The Bible can guide you to be a better person. Each day in all sorts of situations and circumstances we have a choice of whether we do what is right and good, or whether we act selfishly and do wrong. By regularly reading the Bible it reminds us of the best way to live our lives. Each of us needs a constant reminder of the way we should behave. The more we get to know and understand God's message to us in the Bible, the better equipped we will be to live a life that is of real quality and value. Living without the Bible is like throwing away the instructions to a piece of machinery. Or it is like a builder destroying the architect's plans for a building. The Bible is God's guide book for your life and mine. Know what it says and stick to it and you will not go wrong.

The Bible can inspire you

Immanuel Kant, the great philosopher, was a very learned and intelligent man, but the amazing thing is that he once said, 'a single line in the Bible has consoled me more than all the books I have ever read'. He did not say which line in particular comforted and inspired him, rather I think he was making the point that one word from God is worth more than a million words from man. The wonderful thing is that the living God wants to communicate to you, and the way he often does that is through the Bible. There will be times, if you make reading a habit, when a sentence or passage will strike you like the sun bursting through on a cloudy day or like a refreshing cold drink on a hot and dry afternoon.

I remember the first occasion I read the story of Jesus turning the water into wine at the wedding feast at Cana in Galilee. I had not been a Christian for very long, so while I had heard the story before I had never read it myself.

But I will never forget the impact the story had when I realized that part of the meaning of the story was that Jesus wanted to change our lives from being like ordinary water to something special and rich as wine. God wants to change and go on changing our lives for the better. That is good news!

The Bible can challenge you

It is important to have something worthwhile to aim for, something that is a challenge. Can you imagine how awful it would be not to have something to look forward to or aspire to? Life would lack a great deal of meaning and purpose. The Bible is a very challenging book. Some people find it rather threatening to read because it provokes you to think and consider difficult issues which some folk would rather ignore. The Bible challenges the way you and I think and behave, it causes us to consider other people and ask ourselves whether we have the right priorities. It gives us something to aim for because it paints a picture of a way of life that is built on love and faith, and then challenges us to live that way. You cannot set yourself any higher or better goal than to live according to the life-style the Bible shows you. The great saints of the church have become saints simply because they have taken the Bible and its message seriously, and it has transformed their lives as a result. The Bible can transform your life, and you will not find a better instruction book on how to live.

The Bible can warn you of danger

Can you remember how, when you were a small child, your mother would warn you of something that was too hot to touch? So she would tell you not to go too near a fire, or to avoid the cooker. In the same way, by showing you the difference between right and wrong the Bible is able to help you to steer clear of the consequences of making the wrong decisions. It shows us very clearly that speaking the truth and doing what is right is always the best thing to do, and by reading it the Bible encourages us to continue on the right path. One of the wonderful verses in the Psalms says:

'Your word is a lamp to guide me and a light to my path' (Psalm 119:105).

If we stick to the advice that the Bible gives and take note of its guidance then we can avoid all sorts of trouble and mistakes.

I have said that the Bible can guide and inspire you, it can challenge you and direct you on the right path. The Bible can in fact allow God to speak to you in all sorts of ways and in many different circumstances. It is full of a wealth of truth and encouragement, and listed below are some passages you might like to look at and which I'm sure you will find of help.

Passages from the Bible to read when . . .

You are afraid

Psalm 34
Isaiah 41:10
Mark 4:35–41

You are worried or anxious

Psalm 46
Isaiah 43:1–3
Matthew 6:25–34
Philippians 4:6 and 7

You feel far from God

Psalm 42:5–11
Psalm 139:1–18

You are depressed or discouraged

Romans 8:28–39
Hebrews 12:1–3
1 Peter 4:12 and 13

You are doubting

Mark 9:23 and 24
John 20:24–29

Friends let you down

Psalm 27:10–14
Psalm 41
Luke 17:3 and 4

You need guidance

Proverbs 3:5 and 6
Psalm 32:8–10

Isaiah 30:19–21
John 16:12 and 13

You feel guilty

Psalm 51
John 3:16 and 17
1 John 1:5–10

You are lonely

Psalm 23
John 14:15–21
Revelation 3:20

You are thankful

Psalm 92:1–5
Psalm 100
Ephesians 5:18–20

How to read the Bible

Firstly, get hold of a Bible that you find easy to read. In your confirmation classes you may have used a Good News Bible (GNB), if you enjoy that translation then stick with it. But find a version that suits you and one that seems to make things clearer rather than make matters obscure. The New International Version (NIV) is also very popular. If you have a Bible that is your personal copy then after a while you become familiar with it, and it is easier to find a passage or remember where a particular verse occurs.

I also find it helpful to underline in red a verse which has especially struck me or made me think. If you took a look at my Bible you would find that some books have a lot of verses underlined, and that of course makes them easier to find again. Verses that may have a special meaning and value for you are probably worth learning. Set yourself a goal, if you like, to learn ten verses within six months.

You may find Bible reading notes to be a helpful guide. These are notes which choose for you set readings for each day of the week. Take a look at your church bookstall to see if they have any for sale, or speak to your Vicar and ask him what he recommends. I know many teenagers who find reading notes very helpful because they set out the passages for you and they often supply useful thoughts and comments about the text. Another way is to choose a book which you want to look at. Take for example Mark's Gospel. It is the shortest of the four Gospels with only sixteen chapters. You could decide to read a third of each chapter every few days and make a few brief notes about what the passage actually says and what you can learn from it.

You may also find it useful to have a concordance, a reference book which helps you find a passage or verse when you cannot remember where it occurs in the Bible. I use a concordance all the time because I've got an awful memory. I can often remember a few words from a passage but will not have a clue as to where it is located. The great advantage of a concordance is that you can look up the word and it will give you all the references to it, which makes it very easy to find the passage.

It is also helpful to have a Bible handbook which can give you some very useful background information to a book. It will tell you who the author is, when and where it was written, what were the circumstances of the people to whom the book was addressed. In fact a good handbook can give you all sorts of details which help to make the passage more interesting. Go into your local bookshop and have a look around to see what they have got, and if you cannot afford a concordance or handbook, put it on your request list for a birthday or Christmas present.

When should I read my Bible?

The easiest time to read your Bible is when you have also set aside a few spare moments to pray. I think I nearly always read my Bible first and then say my prayers. It can be helpful to ask God in our prayers to give us the strength and ability to put into action the lessons we have learnt from the passage we have just read.

As to what time of day is best, there are no hard and fast rules. If you are a morning person, read it in the morning; if you are a night owl, reading it before you go to sleep might be best for you. The key thing is to make a promise to set aside a special time each day to read God's word and encounter him. It isn't something that comes naturally, I'm afraid, and all sorts of distractions will crop up and get in the way of our Bible reading. That is why it helps to set aside a definite time, the same as you do when you have to wash your hair or do your homework. Inevitably, there will be disturbances at times which we cannot avoid, and there will be periods when we do not regularly read the Bible. But God is not a tyrant, he does not get angry with us over little things. He is loving and understanding and he will always welcome us. When you sit down to read your Bible or to pray, have in your mind a picture of the father that Jesus told a story about, *running* to meet and welcome his prodigal son (Luke 15). That is exactly how God loves us!

What others have said about the Bible

'I know the Bible is inspired because it inspires me.' (Dwight Moody)

'This great book . . . is the best gift God has given to man . . . But for it we could not know right from wrong.' (Abraham Lincoln)

'I read my Bible to know what people ought to do, and my newspaper to know what they are doing.' (Cardinal Newman)

'God's Road Map – the Bible.' (Kenyon Palmer)

'The Bible grows more beautiful, as we grow in our understanding of it.' (von Goethe)

'The New Testament is the best book the world has ever known or will know.' (Charles Dickens)

'Other books were given for our information, the Bible was given for our transformation.' (Anon)

'After more than sixty years of almost daily reading of the Bible, I never fail to find it always new and marvellously in tune with the changing needs of every day'. (Cecil B. De Mille)

'There is a Book worth all other books which were ever printed.' (Patrick Henry)

'The Bible is God's chart for you to steer by, to keep you from the bottom of the sea, and to show you where the harbour is, how to reach it without running on the rocks.' (Henry Beecher)

'The Bible is the one Book to which any thoughtful man may go with any honest question of life or destiny and find the answer of God by honest searching.' (John Ruskin)

CHAPTER EIGHT

Talking Together – Prayer

Prayer is wonderful. Men and women down the centuries have discovered that prayer is a very crucial part of life. Without prayer, life can be very hard and dry. But when we pray something very special happens which we may not always be aware of. We are allowing God to come particularly close and we share with him the things which are of real concern to us. In a way we are allowing God to look into our hearts and our innermost feelings. We are sharing ourselves with him. When we allow God to come close to us and when we look at him then we see our lives in the right perspective, and this breathes spiritual life back into us. It brings us alive again and puts us in touch with God in a fresh way. Prayer can make such a difference and no one can expect to live the Christian life without making prayer a priority. So what is prayer all about?

Prayer begins with God. It is he who is our Father in Heaven and the one who knows us by name and loves us. He has made us his children, and therefore if we want our relationship with him to grow we need to talk to him. You cannot expect any friendship to develop if you do not talk to the person concerned. You have probably experienced with some of your friends that if you do not keep up with them by talking, phoning and seeing each other, then your relationship will drift apart. It can be very difficult, as you may know, when you move house. At first you are very keen to keep in touch with friends from where you previously lived, but as time goes on inevitably the strength of your friendship can weaken.

So if we want to keep our faith and friendship with our Father strong we need to talk frequently with him. We need to keep in touch. Prayer begins with God because it is he who first offered his friendship to us. He wants to come alongside us and share his love with us day by day. You may have a special friend whose company you really value and enjoy. When something happens or you have some particular news they are the first person you want to tell. In many ways this is how God feels about us. He is delighted when we come to him, and he is anxious to give his love to us through our friends, through the gifts we may have and the things we enjoy. If you look at the beauty of creation you can see that God is trying to communicate to us that he has given us a special world to live in, a world of colour and light and amazing complexity and variety. When he created the colour green God was not content to have all the fields and trees of one shade. Instead, because of his infinite imagination, he gave us more variety of that one colour than we would have been capable of thinking of. It is this God who is concerned for both the great and the small, the finite and the infinite, who wants us to renew our friendship with him day by day by sharing our thoughts and prayers with him. Prayer begins with us recognizing all that God has done for us in creation and salvation. The sad thing is that we often spoil the things he gives to us. But he does not reject us because of that, but rather calls us to come closer to him and live our lives the way that is best and the way that he originally intended.

Prayer is simply talking to God. It is focusing our thoughts and minds on him. When you talk to someone you turn and face them and look at them. You give them your attention. You look at them and they look at you. Prayer is turning towards God.

Prayer brings you closer to God because there are just the two of you talking together. It can be a very personal and intimate experience.

Have you ever had an audience with the Queen at Buckingham Palace? You will probably say No and it is not very likely that you ever will. However, you never know. One day in the future you may be called to the Palace for something special you have done. Who can tell what may happen in the years to come? If you do go for an audience you would not expect just to drift in and pull up a chair. You would come in reverently, acknowledging whose presence you were in. In the same way, when Jesus taught his disciples to pray he said that we should first acknowledge who God is. That is why he said we should begin by saying, 'Our Father who art in heaven, hallowed be your name . . . '. In other words, we acknowledge that it is God who is our Father and Creator, and because of that his name is to be praised and revered. He is our Lord and Ruler who is concerned about us and welcomes us into his presence, so we should give him the respect that he deserves. God is indeed our friend who is always with us but we should never treat him disrespectfully. We should always be mindful of who he is.

What should we pray about?

Well, what should we talk to God about? Of course about our concerns, but we should begin by giving thanks for all that he has done for us. There are plenty of things we can thank him for – our life, food, health, parents, friends, and family. There will always be something positive, something good we can give thanks for, even when life seems very difficult and painful. In fact if you give just a little thought you can probably think of a multitude of things, both great and small, that it is worth saying thank you for.

There is nothing worse than someone who is ungrateful. If you have ever experienced a friend who takes you for granted and never appreciates what you do for them, you will know how difficult it is. It may not be that you want any sort of praise for what you do for them, but just a thank-you would be really appreciated. How do you think God feels at times when we do not show any sort of appreciation or gratitude? I'm sure he feels pained about it. This is why it is important that we give thanks to God. So make time in your prayers to say 'Thank You'. Show your appreciation to God in the way you most enjoy. You do not have to be quiet and serious if you do not want to be. I'm sure that the worship in heaven is not always quiet.

Have you ever been to a pop concert? I expect that you will say yes, or at least that you hope to go one day. The great thing about concerts is that they are usually very noisy affairs with a lot of energy, lights and enthusiasm. You become caught up in the whole experience. You can feel the music and it is almost as if you can see the sound hit the roof and reverberate about the building. I'm sure that the worship in heaven is often like a concert, full of energy and vibrancy.

God wants us to worship him, sometimes quietly and reverently but sometimes with a loud voice as well. We may at times feel we want to shout his praises from the rooftops, thanking him for all he has done for us. If you feel that way at times do not think that it is inappropriate, because look at what the Psalms say:

> Clap your hands, all peoples!
> Shout to God with loud songs of joy
> For the Lord, the Most High, is terrible,
> a great king over all the earth.

If in your prayers you want to shout your thanks to God, then do it. Mind you, it might be diplomatic to make sure that you will not disturb someone else in doing so!

What should you do next?

Pray for your family and friends

Being part of a family can be very difficult
at times. Arguments can start over the most
stupid of issues and members can say things
that are very hurtful. Your parents may be
divorced, which can be painful, or possibly
you feel your parents do not understand each
other and often do not understand you. Praying for your family can be a very positive
thing to do, because it helps us to see our
parents and brothers and sisters in the way
that God sees them. It can help us understand
a difficult situation and how we should
handle it. But it is not good enough to pray
and then do nothing, prayer should always
lead to action. If your prayer is that things
should be better at home, then start making
them better by being helpful and co-oper-
ative.

Pray for your Mum. Pray that God may
bless and strengthen her in all the work that
she has to do. Ask that your relationship with
her may grow and deepen, that you may have
a better understanding between you. Then
try to make life easier for her by offering some
practical help. Make your bed. Tidy your
room. Ease the hassle that makes things difficult at times. As one Christian said, 'Pray,
then start answering your prayers'.

Pray for your Dad. Things may have been

129

difficult at work, with various pressures and important decisions that have to be made. It is not easy at times. Work can involve a lot of stress because of all the various responsibilities your Dad may have. Pray for him, and take the trouble to find out what he may be concerned about. If it is appropriate, ask him what he would like you to pray for, that can be a great help. Pray also that your relationship may improve and grow stronger. Dads as well as Mums are very special, so they deserve your understanding and your prayers. You may not get on well with your parents at times and things may be quite difficult at home. But prayer can help. It can help you see your parents as God sees them and in a better light. It can help you understand what they feel. It is actually not easy being a parent. It can be very hard work, and sometimes you do not make it any easier. So show your love and care and ask God to bless your family.

Then there are your friends and their ups and downs. It's great to have friends. Life would be terrible without them, though at times you may think you would be better off! But just imagine if there was no one to share things with and to talk to. Life would be very cold and lonely. So pray for them and the things that concern them. Prayer can be so important because it strengthens our relationship with our friends. It shows that we are thinking of them and wish that only good should come their way. Prayer can make a relationship special, and it's great to be able to pray for our friends because of the strength and help it can give to them. You may also find it helpful to get together with a friend once a week, or possibly once a month, and pray together. Jesus promised that where two or three are gathered together in his name then he would be in the midst of them. So when two of you agree to pray together, Jesus is with you, and praying together can be very helpful and effective. Why not try it?

Lord, I'm sorry

Prayer is also concerned with saying sorry. Sometimes you may not tell the truth or deliberately distort things to get out of a difficult situation. You may, like all of us, be unkind and selfish to others. When this is the case we cannot come to God in prayer as if nothing has happened, rather we need to ask God to forgive us. If we say we are Christians and yet we do not live a Christian life, then we are betraying ourselves and the God we believe in. It is good to stop for a few moments in your prayers and recall the things you know that you have done wrong. Possibly you were bad-tempered with someone or said something cruel behind someone's back. Maybe your thoughts were filled with sexual fantasies which you know were wrong. All these things we need to confess to God and ask him to forgive us. If we allow our sins and wrong-doing to go without confessing them to God, then they will spoil our relationship with him. However, if we tell God what we have done wrong then the wonderful thing is that he will forgive us. We need not then walk around with a continual feeling of guilt, because once God has forgiven us he does not hold our sins against us, in fact he forgets about them completely. No matter what we have done or how bad it is, God will forgive us if we ask him, and because he forgives us he wants us to forgive others.

Praying for the world

It is important in your prayers to look beyond your own horizons and think of those in the wider world. Traditionally in church we pray for the Queen and members of her government as well as the world leaders, that there may be peace and co-operation between peoples and nations. In your own prayers remember the people you have seen on television or read about in the newspaper who particularly need prayer because of something that may have happened to them. Often when I'm watching the news I pray for the people I see who have suffered some tragedy, or I pray for the families of someone who has been killed. I remember on one occasion feeling very strongly that I should pray for someone who was shown on the news and who had been a victim of a terrorist attack. Fortunately the man survived, but afterwards I discovered that the man was a Christian, which made me realize that my strong feelings were God's way of encouraging me to pray for a fellow brother in need.

At times we may pray for all sorts of terrible things that happen in the world, and wonder whether our prayers have any effect at all. For example, millions of Christians have prayed for various troubled areas of the world for many years, and yet people are still being murdered and still hate each other. You cannot easily identify how and why prayer is helpful, but if we feel prayer is effective on a personal level then we can believe that it is helpful on an international level as well. If you pray for a part of the world where there is famine and that motivates you to give some money toward famine relief, then you have answered your own prayers. Also prayer is often part of the process of understanding and thinking about a problem and then knowing what to do to solve it. Also, pray for those who are working to relieve suffering.

Because praying is a spiritual activity it can spiritually encourage and strengthen those who you are praying for.

Making space for prayer

Prayer is also about being quiet at times. Things may be noisy at home, so where do you go to be quiet? If you are fortunate to have your own bedroom then it may not be a problem to get a little bit of privacy. But let me make a few other suggestions which you might find helpful if it is difficult to find space at home to pray.

— Going for a walk can provide the opportunity to be alone to think, reflect and pray. Is there a park or pleasant walk near you which would be suitable?

— Take off on your bicycle to somewhere where you know you will not be disturbed.

— One very easy way of finding space is to drop into church. You will usually find that one of the side chapels is an excellent spot to do some thinking and praying. If your church is often kept locked, ask your Vicar if you can borrow the key. He probably would be delighted to know that you wanted to use the church.

If you give it a little bit of thought you can probably think of quite a number of times and places where you can go to be quiet and alone

134

with God. Jesus would often try to get away from the vast crowds that followed him so that he could have the opportunity to pray. It is amazing in many ways, because it is so tempting to fill our lives with being busy all the time, particularly if people need our help. Despite the fact that Jesus was desperately needed and sought by so many people, he realized that it was of crucial importance to go and spend time with his Father. If Jesus needed those times with God when he could renew his spiritual strength, then you and I need them too.

One problem about making space for God is not just finding the time and place, that can be easy if we get our priorities right, but how to keep our minds on our prayers. Sometimes when I start to pray I suddenly find my mind invaded by a dozen other thoughts of things I need to do or something I've forgotten. It is a common problem which I'm sure you have experienced as well. I find it helpful, if my thoughts are wandering all over the place, to hold a cross in my hands. If you do not have a cross of your own, make one. If it is just a very simple cross of two pieces of wood you have put together then that would be suitable. Some friends of mine find it helpful to light a candle and to watch the flames as they pray. It gives them a sense of peace and reminds them of the serenity of God.

Mind you, if you do use a candle it might be diplomatic to have a word with your mother beforehand, in case she is anxious about any accidents.

It is good to have somewhere to pray that is quiet and where we can be alone with our thoughts, but prayers can be said anywhere, at any time. There is nothing to stop you praying as you walk along the corridor at school or on the way home on the bus. Prayers can be said anywhere. They do not have to be said with your eyes closed or when you are kneeling. I often pray when I am driving along in the car. Closing your eyes then is not recommended!

Listening to God

Prayer is basically talking to God but it is also about listening to God as well. You may say, 'Don't be crazy, how can you listen to God? Only people who are mad claim that God speaks to them.' Was Moses mad or Abraham or St Paul? There may be times in our Christian lives when, like some of the characters of the Bible, we hear the voice of God. You may have already experienced that. God does speak to his children and we need to listen. How then do you discern between what are your own thoughts and what is the Spirit of God leading and directing you? Firstly, nothing that contradicts the teachings of the Bible will be from God. So if you feel that God is speaking to you, check it out with what the Bible says. Secondly, ask someone who is more spiritually mature and is in a leadership position in your church whether they agree with what you think God is saying. You could ask your youth group leader, the churchwarden or your Vicar. I'm sure they would be happy to help and advise. God does not speak to people just for their own benefit, so never go and do something on your own. If you feel God is calling you to help with the Sunday School, or start a prayer group, or be involved in some act of service, then always talk to someone else about it.

You may still ask the question, How do we listen to God? God is love. We grow in our Christian lives as we learn to love God and to love others. If we do something that denies that love, such as being selfish or immoral, then the voice of God through our conscience will tell us that we are wrong. We will feel uncomfortable and lacking in God's peace. That is God speaking, showing you that love and friendship is greater and stronger than greed and selfishness. Let me put it another way. When you see something beautiful it makes you feel good and inspires you. God is beautiful. In fact he is more beautiful than any precious stone or diamond ring. He is more beautiful than any snow-capped mountain or lush green valley. So he speaks to us and inspires us not only through the beauty of all the created things, but through the friendship of others and through the care he shows us through Jesus his son. Jesus shows us what God is like. He came to show us what is good and true. So if you want God to speak to you, look at all the beautiful things in life and the powerful things such as trust, love, truth, honesty and faith. And most of all, look at Jesus because he shows us by his words and actions what he is calling us to do today in his world.

Listening to God in our prayers is very important. It also takes time and experience to know how to discern the voice of God. Talk to your Vicar or youth group leader about it and don't be afraid to ask any awkward or difficult questions.

Help! Prayer is difficult

I hope I have not given you the impression that prayer is always wonderful and an easy thing to do. You probably know that it is not. Prayer is difficult. Often you are tired, you have been under a lot of pressure and you do not feel like praying. It is easy to skip praying one day, and then before you realize it a week has gone by and you have not done any serious talking to God. There can also be times when our routine is upset, such as exams, family holidays, illness, moving house – to mention just a few reasons. Virtually every Christian I know, including myself, has gone through times when they have not prayed. So if you feel a failure at times because you have forgotten your prayers, then join the company! However, if we realize that we have not given prayer the priority that it should have in our lives, the thing is not to give up due to guilt, but rather to start again. You can do that by setting yourself achievable goals. Aim to pray every day for five minutes. Don't feel you have to measure up to other people's spiritual achievements. If they pray for twenty minutes every day – fine. But that does not mean you are a failure if you only pray for five. There is nothing worse than setting out with unrealistic expectations of what you are going to do, and then not being able to stick to them. So be reasonable. Try to make the effort to pray for a period of time you know you can manage. Even if it is only for two minutes, that is better than not praying at all.

There will be occasions when prayer comes very easily and you think that you have got it worked out. But there will come times when it will be very difficult and you will feel that you are doing it out of duty. This is a normal Christian experience. The important thing is not to give up but to be persistent. Often the most worthwhile things in life have to be worked at because they do not come without effort. So stick with it, the benefits and value are enormous!

Some brief guidelines on prayer

THE PLACE – Can be anywhere, but best when you are alone.

THE TIME – Up to you. First thing in the morning or last thing at night. Basically any time you like, but try to make it regular.

WHO DO YOU PRAY TO? – God your Heavenly Father who loves you and cares about you. He invites you into his presence.

WHAT DO YOU SAY? – What ever you like. However, it is good to express your thanks and mention your family and friends. Say sorry for the things you know you have done wrong, and finally express whatever is concerning or worrying you.

DO YOU HAVE TO KNEEL? – No. You can stand or sit. It does not matter what posture you are in when you pray. You can pray with your eyes open or closed, there is no strict rule.

HOW DO I LISTEN TO GOD? – By knowing the truth of God's love and seeking to obey his will in all things.

DOES IT WORK? – The important thing about prayer is not getting God to do things for you but discovering what he wants you do do for him.

DOES GOD ALWAYS ANSWER PRAYER? – Yes, but God does not always give the answers that we want. He always acts to do what in the long term is the best for us. We cannot dictate to God what he should do. Remember, even Jesus asked his Father if he could avoid the cross, but God said No. Often we look for the easy answer to a problem. But God's ways are not our ways. All we can do at times is just trust him.

What others have said about prayer

'Seven days without prayer makes one weak.' (Allen Bartlett)

'If you are swept off your feet, it's time to get on your knees.' (Fred Beck)

'Prayer, in its simplest definition, is merely a wish turned God-ward.' (Phillip Brooks)

'If you would have God hear you when you pray, you hear him when he speaks.' (Thomas Brooks)

'Prayer is conversation with God.' (Clement of Alexandria)

'Pray and then start answering your prayer.' (Deane Edwards)

'Prayer does not change God, but changes him who prays.' (Soren Kierkegaard)

'The fewer the words the better the prayer.' (Martin Luther)

'Prayer opens our eyes that we may see ourselves and others as God sees us.' (Clara Palmer)

'Prayer is dangerous business, results do come.' (Christie Swain)

'Prayer at its highest is a two-way conversation – and for me the most important part is listening to God's replies.' (Frank Raubach)

Some prayers worth learning

It is always worthwhile knowing a number of
prayers which you can use when it is appropriate. This can be helpful when you are not
sure of what to say and when you cannot
find the right words to express what you feel.
Here are three prayers which you may find
helpful, but I suggest that you find a number
which you particularly like and learn them.

Day by day, dear Lord, of thee
Three things we pray:
To see thee more clearly;
To love thee more dearly;
To follow thee more nearly;
Day by day. Amen (St Richard of Chich-
ester)

O gracious and Holy Father,
Give us wisdom to see you,
intelligence to understand you,
diligence to seek you,
patience to wait for you,
eyes to behold you,
a heart to meditate upon you,
and a life to proclaim you,
through the power of the Spirit of
Jesus Christ our Lord. Amen.
(St Benedict)

Being Confirmed

Eternal God and Father,
you create us by your power
and redeem us by your love:
guide and strengthen us by your Spirit,
that we may give ourselves in love and
service
to one another and to you;
through Jesus Christ our Lord. Amen.
Alternative Service Book (A.S.B.)

CHAPTER NINE

Christian Living

A number of years ago two friends got together one winter's evening for dinner. One was a vicar and the other was a farmer. After they had finished their meal they sat beside the fire talking. Eventually they began to talk about being a Christian in today's world, with all its pressures and hassles. The farmer asked his friend, 'Do you really think it is necessary to go to church?' The vicar, without saying a word, got up from his chair, picked up a pair of tongs, and lifted one of the coals out of the fire and put it in front of the hearth. They both sat there in silence and watched the piece of coal lose its red glow and eventually go out. The vicar then got up, picked up the coal, put it back in the fire and they watched it slowly ignite and regain its bright red glow. The farmer said, 'I take your point'.

If we want our confirmed faith in God to be strong. If we want God to be real to us and know the power and strength of his Spirit, then you must not go it alone. With the best will in the world you will find that your commitment and enthusiasm will gradually be worn down if you do not have the help and encouragement of other Christians. If you want the glow and warmth of your faith to be strong, stay where the inspiration and encouragement can be found.

Christian living is about being part of the family of God, and it is also about living as a child of God. Let me ask you a direct question. What is the difference between someone who is a Christian and someone who is not a Christian? Is it that the Christian is better than the person who is not? Are they nicer or necessarily kinder? Not at all. There are many people who are not Christians who are just as kind and thoughtful, in fact they may even be much better people. Essentially the difference is that to be a Christian is to be a child, and not to be a Christian is to be an orphan. A Christian is a child of God, someone who knows that they have a heavenly Father who loves them and cares for them. They have a relationship which is special and unique. Your relationship to God is your Father's love for you and your friendship with him. Sadly, someone who is not a Christian has not got that friendship. As far as they are concerned God does not exist, or at least, if he does they have never met him. They have never opened the door to the one who has been constantly knocking at the entrance of their lives asking if he can come in to be a friend.

You are a child of your heavenly Father, therefore go and live your life as a child who will not bring shame to their Dad but rather will make him feel proud. You may feel that your relationship with your parents is not always easy. However, your parents are happy when you are fulfilled in something that you want to do. They have your best interests at heart and they want you to do well, whether it is in your school work, sports, hobbies or your job. God your Father has something of the same relationship. He wants the best for you. When you find things hard and painful, he is concerned and cares. When you are happy and things are going well, he is pleased. When you are disobedient and selfish, he is hurt and ashamed of you, but he never rejects you. In fact, just as I have been writing this piece of the last chapter a mum has phoned me about her son. It was not an easy phone call, because the mother was in tears. Her son had just been dismissed from his job, and his future is not looking good. I am sure that at times God weeps over us, at times he laughs, at times he cheers and claps; after all he is our Father. You and I then should be resolved to live our lives as a child obeying our Father who has our best interests at heart. Christian living is about building our lives on the firm foundation of God's commands. Living according to the maker's instructions!

What advice then does God give?

OUR LORD JESUS CHRIST SAID, IF YOU LOVE ME, KEEP MY COMMANDMENTS; HAPPY ARE THOSE WHO HEAR THE WORD OF GOD AND KEEP IT. HEAR THEN THESE COMMAND-MENTS WHICH GOD HAS GIVEN TO HIS PEOPLE, AND TAKE THEM TO HEART.

I AM THE LORD YOUR GOD: YOU SHALL HAVE NO OTHER GODS BUT ME.

You shall love the Lord your God with all your heart, with all your soul, with all your mind, and with all your strength.

God demands all of our love simply because he has given us all of his love. He is the one who has created us and given us life. Without him we would not exist or have any real reason or ultimate purpose for living. He has been the scapegoat for us by dying on the cross and accepting the responsibility for our sin. He is our God, and our relationship with him is based not on fear but on an act of will where we have decided to show our gratitude by responding to his love for us by loving him.

YOU SHALL NOT MAKE FOR YOURSELF ANY IDOL

God is spirit, and those who worship him must worship in spirit and in truth.

There should be no other focus of our worship but God. The Bible tells us that God is a jealous God who permits no rivals. Nothing else compares with God so we must take care that no person or object gets in the way of our relationship with him. It is very easy for material possessions to assume a greater importance than they should have. It is also easy to allow money to dominate our values. Sometimes we can become enslaved to our own ambition and we become the centre of our world, and other people cease to matter. But do not misunderstand me, there is nothing wrong with possessions or money or ambition in themselves, it is, however, that we can run the risk of letting them become of all-consuming importance. Loving God and doing his will should be the ultimate priority in our lives and should govern the way that we conduct ourselves.

YOU SHOULD NOT DISHONOUR THE NAME OF THE LORD YOUR GOD.

You shall worship him with awe and reverence.

How would you feel if people used your name as a swear word? Upset? It would not be a very pleasant experience. Yet how often do you hear the word 'God' or 'Christ' used as a swear word? If you respect someone you treat their name with care. So also God. It is very easy to use the same words that everyone around you is using, but as Christians we are called to be self-controlled. In other words, we should only allow ourselves to do the things which we know are right. If you can control what you say then you will be able to control what you do. I am often aware of saying things which I should not, and I feel bad when I have abused the name of my best friend. Some people will say that it does not matter. But God says it does. So all of us should treat his name with respect.

REMEMBER THE LORD'S DAY AND KEEP IT HOLY.

Christ is risen from the dead: set your minds on the things that are above, not on the things that are on the earth.

We have already discussed this very important commandment in our chapter on Holy Communion, and the story I told you at the beginning of this chapter illustrates the importance of regular worship. God knows what is best for us, so do not ignore the rules.

HONOUR YOUR FATHER AND MOTHER.

Live as servants of God; honour all men; love the brotherhood.

Your relationship with your parents is obviously very important. There may be periods when you get on very well together, and there may be times when things are very tense and difficult. As a Christian your duty is to obey your parents. In the majority of cases that is probably what you do, but you may feel at times that they are putting unreasonable demands and restrictions on you. What can be helpful is if you try to see things from their point of view. They will not ask you to do something if they do not think it is for your own good. Your parents, because they gave birth to you, nurtured you and brought you up, naturally feel protective towards you. They do not want you to get into any sort of trouble. Most of your conflict with your parents is probably because you want to assert your own independence and be more of your own boss. There is nothing wrong with that, because eventually you will leave home and set up your own life and possibly start a family. However, the period now for you as a teenager can be difficult because you are still establishing your own views and becoming an adult yourself. Any change causes conflict and it may cause conflict for you at home. It needs a great deal of maturity to understand what is happening in your changing relationship with your parents, and then have the courage to accept that you are still their responsibility. Giving honour to your parents means giving them the respect that they deserve and co-operating with them when they ask you to do something. Whether your parents are practising Christians or not, the best way you can serve God in your family is by co-operating with your parents. It is easy to be a good Christian at church with activities you are involved in there, or with your friends, but being a Christian at home requires a great deal of patience and love. If you find it difficult, pray about it and try to talk with your parents and brothers and sisters. A lot of conflict is due to misunderstandings, and if you can overcome that by talking and really communicating then you will be most of the way towards solving the problem.

YOU SHALL NOT COMMIT MURDER.

Be reconciled to your brother, overcome evil with good.

Life is sacred. Our physical life ends at death

but our spiritual life continues as we experience the presence of God in a fuller sense. But all life is a gift from God, and only God has the right to allow life to end. That is why we should never take our own or anyone else's life into our own hands. It is not ours to give and therefore it is not ours to take.

There are times when, due to injustice and attack from another nation, there is no alternative but to go to war, but this does not undermine the basic rule that you should never murder.

YOU SHALL NOT COMMIT ADULTERY.

Know that your body is a temple of the Holy Spirit.

You may have experienced the trauma of your parents' divorce, or you will know a friend who has been through the awful ordeal. It may not necessarily have been either your mum's or dad's fault, but the Christian ideal has always been that marriage is for life. At times all of us fail to live up to the ideals which we may have.

The appropriate place for sex is within the relationship of the long-term commitment of marriage. People around you may say that the Christian view of sex is out of date and is rather Victorian. But the Christian understanding is the most up-to-date view, because

153

it is based on values that do not change according to the latest fashion. Sex is for marriage. Sex outside marriage is called fornication if you are not married, or adultery if you are. To commit adultery is a terrible betrayal of your husband or wife, and is one of the worst breaches of another person's trust in you.

But why does Christianity say that sex is only for marriage? The basic reason is because if you consider all the issues involved, it makes sense. From a medical viewpoint to have sex with more than one partner increases the risk of sexually transmitted disease. Sexual diseases are the body's way of saying that it should not be treated in that way. We were not designed to have sex other than with our life-long partner.

From an emotional viewpoint sex needs to be in the right context. If it happens before there is a real commitment from each partner then you run the danger that it obscures your genuine feelings of friendship. Sex raises the physical side of a friendship and may make the whole relationship far too emotional unless the two persons have a deep understanding of each other. The danger can often be that sex is merely reduced to the level of physical pleasure, so that one partner can be using the other and they are appreciated for not much more than just their body.

It is argued by many that it is good to have sex before marriage because it enables you to discover whether you are sexually compatible with your partner. If this argument was true it would mean that marriages would be more secure and lasting. Sadly the evidence points in the opposite direction. Having sex before marriage does not produce a more stable relationship.

Many girls are faced with pressure from boys to have sex, and it is a common belief that if a girl wishes to have a boyfriend then she has got to be prepared to sleep with him. But for you as a girl, or indeed a boy, if your friend is putting pressure on you to have sex and that is not what you feel is right, then stand your ground and do not be afraid to say – No! If they then give up on your friendship because you say no, do they really want you for a friend or just for your body?

It also makes sense to keep sex within the permanent relationship of marriage because it has consequences. The most obvious consequence of sex is pregnancy. There is no one hundred per cent safe form of contraceptive, and pregnancy is always a possibility with having a sexual relationship. One Christian recently said, 'One of life's greatest accomplishments is getting love, marriage and sex in the right order with the right person at the right time'. It is not easy but it is worth getting it right.

Sex is a gift from God. It is something wonderful and good, but like anything of value it needs to be handled with care. The intention is that this special gift should be for marriage and if someone has already had sex before, then they have nothing unique to give to their partner. The Christian understanding that sex is only for marriage makes good sense. Think about it very carefully because it is such an important issue.

YOU SHALL NOT STEAL.

Be honest in all that you do and care for those in need.

Taking something that belongs to someone else is wrong. If an item does not belong to you then it is not yours for the taking. Just think about it – if people chose to ignore this commandment it would be only a matter of weeks before society and commerce collapsed. Shops would go out of business because they would be unable to buy and sell and make a profit. Jobs would be lost and anarchy would prevail.

To be honest and respect other people's property makes good sense, because you want to preserve what you possess. But it is not just for self-interest, it is for the general well-being and order of everyone.

YOU SHALL NOT BE A FALSE WITNESS.

Let everyone speak the truth.

This commandment is like the previous one. If you were unable to trust what people said then chaos would come about. As a Christian you should always strive to tell the truth. At times that may be difficult and will not be popular. It is often easier to tell a lie and get out of a short-term problem. But lying in the end solves nothing. It is far better being a person who is known for their honesty and truthfulness. Others will respect you and will know where they stand, because they realize that what you say can be trusted. It is only weak-minded people who lie and it does them no good.

YOU SHALL NOT COVET ANYTHING WHICH BELONGS TO YOUR NEIGHBOUR.

Remember the words of the Lord Jesus: It is more blessed to give than to receive. Love your neighbour as yourself, for love is the fulfilling of the law.

The first question you may ask is, What does 'covet' mean? Covet is an old word which basically means to envy. But it means something more than that, in that it means envy to the extent that you want to take what someone else has got.

It is all right to admire what someone has. That may be a possession such as their house or car. It may be a responsibility they hold at school or college or a personal ability they may have. It becomes a sin when you envy what they have to the extent that you take it from them or undermine their position. Envy and jealousy are dangerous in friendships and they can destroy so much. They are particularly harmful to the person who is committing the sin.

Being confirmed

Christian living is not easy, but Jesus never said it would be. God gives us the best and highest principles and standards to aim for. The exciting thing for you, as someone who has recently been confirmed, is that you can face the future with confidence. You have a wonderful God to lead you and guide you. You may make mistakes and get lost and confused at times, but he will always lead you back to the right way.

Being a Christian is the most worthwhile experience you can have and it changes our life here on earth and affects our life after death. So you see, being confirmed is never the end of a course or something you can put behind you, but rather it is about affirming what you believe and stepping out into the future with a desire to know more of God and to be used by him. Do not make the mistake of thinking that there is no more to discover of God. There is always a lot to discover about a friend, particularly God, and that makes our relationship with him so interesting, stimulating and exciting. So never stop thinking, talking, questioning, and seeking to know more of him and his ways.

I wish you well on your journey, and I

hope that what I have said to you, and all the things that we have looked at, have been helpful.

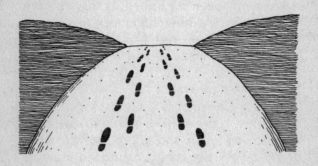